Praise for *Gifted*

'These are deeply inspiring stories that teach us that being grateful for small mercies can transform them into major achievements. More than anything else, it is the attitude of the men and women in *Gifted* that defines what it is to be truly gifted.' **Naseeruddin Shah, actor**

'Lives that raise us above ourselves. Travails that put our little difficulties in perspective. Each life, a reason for hope.' **Arun Shourie, journalist, author, politician**

'Rarely have stories been written that celebrate the extraordinary lives of people who live with disability. The book is a glimpse into their world, where they live with courage, determination, and a zest for life. To read their stories is to know that living in the present, with complete acceptance of who we are, is an ability that can change not just our own lives but that of those around us. A powerful, moving, and inspiring read...for all.' **Nandita Das, actor**

'Incisive, evocative and heart-warming at the same time, *Gifted* is a book all of us should read, for many reasons. Each of the stories shows us the inherent strength of the human spirit when faced with the most formidable challenges. The stories in *Gifted* makes us introspect, count our blessings, inspire us to push our own boundaries, and think of how we can give back to the society, much like the stars of this book do.' **Kiran Bedi, first woman IPS officer; founder, Navjyoti India Foundation**

'At last, we have in the mainstream, stories of people with disabilities. Their narratives, recounted in first person, are not only a source of inspiration but also bring forth the grit and determination that is required to succeed in a difficult and challenging world. The authors need to be appreciated for collating these poignant personal testimonies that makes for compulsive reading. This collection is for the disabled as well as the non-disabled and can help lower many attitudinal barriers. The people featured here are veritable role models from whose trials and triumphs we all can gain insight, even as we celebrate their achievements. Normally, the success stories of people with disabilities have limited circulation within the disability sector. But this book has universal appeal.' **Poonam Natarajan, Chairperson, National Trust (Ministry of Social Justice & Empowerment, Govt. of India)**

'This amazing collection of stories redefines the concept of leadership and illustrates the power of determination. *Gifted* will change your views on what's possible.' **Bill McDermott, CEO, SAP AG**

'Warm, inspiring and full of hope. *Gifted* is a book that each of us needs to read, to know and to fully understand the incredible people who live on this earth with us, often unrecognized and included in our world. To read their stories in this book is to know that we are all the same, except that they are born special in some ways. I will never look at differently-abled people with pity or curiosity ever again. Instead, I will look at them thinking there is a treasure trove of talent and determination residing in that body and mind.' **Kris Gopalakrishnan, co-founder, Infosys Ltd**

'This book is an important milestone in documenting the true journeys and histories of people with disabilities and brings to light their perseverance, determination, and optimism as they refuse to be held back by traditional boundaries and mindsets. Through these stories the authors manage to show us not just the fears but also the hopes, dreams, and aspirations of differently-abled people and the impact of their work on our world.' **Shaheen Mistri, founder and CEO, Teach For India**

'Truly inspiring stories...makes one wonder when and how we lost this sense of honesty that one notices in the people in this book. They are really GIFTED in the true sense.' **Bombay Jayashri Ramnath, classical singer and music composer**

'We often look for inspiration from places considered much above our sphere of influence when true inspiration lies all around us. The exemplary individuals outlined in these pages epitomize this truth perfectly and reading their inspiring stories will leave you with no room for excuses, only cause for action and awe. This book not only acknowledges the indomitable spirit of those who continually defy all odds, but also pays tribute to the quiet strength of those who stand behind scenes bringing out the best of the GIFTED.' **Lakshmi Pratury, curator, INKtalks.com**

'The 15 brave individuals profiled in this book are the 21st century alchemists. They deftly transmuted tremendous adversity in life into an opportunity for personal and collective growth. This inspiring book is an ode to the resilience of human spirit.' **Navi Radjou, co-author of** *Jugaad Innovation* **and** *From Smart To Wise*

GIFTED

Also by Sudha Menon

Legacy

GIFTED

Inspiring Stories of
People with Disabilities

SUDHA MENON
V.R. FEROSE

with gratitude,

EBURY
PRESS

EBURY PRESS

USA | Canada | UK | Ireland | Australia
New Zealand | India | South Africa | China

Ebury Press is part of the Penguin Random House group of companies
whose addresses can be found at global.penguinrandomhouse.com

Published by Penguin Random House India Pvt. Ltd
7th Floor, Infinity Tower C, DLF Cyber City,
Gurgaon 122 002, Haryana, India

Penguin
Random House
India

First published by Random House India 2014

Copyright © Sudha Menon and V.R. Ferose 2014
Illustrations © Nachiket Vinay

All rights reserved

12 11 10 9 8 7 6

ISBN 9788184005455

Typeset in GoudyOlSt BT by R. Ajith Kumar
Printed at Replika Press Pvt. Ltd, India

www.penguin.co.in

To all the people who are growing up in an unequal world which simply does not recognize or celebrate their uniqueness.

All the royalty from the sales of this book will go to Enable India, an organization that works for people with disabilities. Our only objective is to spread awareness and sensitize people about the extraordinary gifts that the wonderful men and women in our book possess. We want people to know that each one of us has a special talent hidden within us and we need to go deep within to pull that gift out and showcase it to the world.

CONTENTS

INTRODUCTION

'Pammi! Pammi!', the high-pitched voice would cut across the thick summer air, from beyond the high compound wall of the house that I grew up in, back in the early 70s. In an instant, the household would come awake, my siblings and I rushing to open the door and welcome our very important visitor—the only person ever who could make my mother give up her afternoon siesta.

Our 'special' visitor would sit cross-legged on the cement floor of our veranda and polish off the treat that she served him: a huge mound of rice, with sambar that he insisted that she pour into a well that he made right in the centre, accompanied by some pickle and the pappadum that we ate with every meal. There is nothing more joyful for a mother than to serve up a meal to a child who relishes every morsel and shows her his appreciation. But it was not a pleasant sight to see him eat. The sambar would spill all over him as he slurped it and the front of his shirt would be stained with red and yellow dribble but we still sat around him as he ate because he made the most amusing conversations, about Amitabh Bachchan and Hema Malini and about the ghost in the neighbourhood who ventured out on lonely nights to chase unsuspecting way farers. At the end of the meal, he would run his hand over his stomach and burp out his appreciation for amma's meal, wash his hands, clean up his shirt front, and leave, promising to visit soon.

I don't remember his name but what I do remember is how startlingly good looking he was, with his tall, lean frame, his shock of curly hair, and brown, trusting eyes, like that of a deer. I must have been barely 8 years old back then but I can't forget how my heart went out to him every time I saw him, lying curled up outside his home, with nothing to protect him from his tormentors. And there were many in the small town that we grew up in. The kids were the cruelest and they tortured him in new and innovative ways. Sometimes they would sneak up to him while he slept and tie an empty can with a long piece of string to his leg. One of them would then creep up and scream into his ear so that he would wake up in terror and start running, the kids screaming with laughter, chasing him as he ran away from an imagined horror, the tin can rattling after him. If it was Diwali season, the tin can would also have some crackers that they set off just before they startled him awake.

Decades later, I still remember the boy even though my memories are now tinged with guilt because there were times that I, as a little girl, had laughed seeing him run away as the kids teased him, or when I saw the red ribbon that somebody had tied on the back of his tattered khakhi shorts flutter merrily after him as he roamed carefree on the streets.

They called him 'yeda' (crazy) but when I look back today, there was nothing crazy about him. He was polite to my mother and very fond of her, occasionally embarrassing her in the neighbourhood market by addressing her as *Pammi*, a nickname that he had made for her. He was cheerful at all times and to my knowledge, never did anything to harm anyone. Maybe he was a slow learner, maybe his IQ was not the same as the rest of us, but he certainly was not mad in the way I know it today.

Throughout the process of writing *Gifted*, I remembered the boy and it hurt when I thought of how different his life would have been if he had been born in another age. Today there is an iPhone and technology that helps people with disability to lead fulfilled lives, such as software that reads out books and email to the visually handicapped, text messages that help the hearing impaired to move around freely etc., and doctors and therapists who will know exactly what is going wrong inside their body and mind; back then, there was nothing. Each time I met one of the wonderful people in this book and heard their unique story, I thought of the boy who spent his life roaming the street, living on the charity of kind-hearted people, because his life never gave him any chances. The men and women in *Gifted* were unconditionally loved and supported by those around them. Their families had faith in them and built their confidence with positive messages. The boy from my childhood had a family who cast him out of their home and their life, giving him a tattered blanket on which he slept, outside his house and he had nothing but the prospect of living as a *yeda*.

My family moved away from suburban Mumbai when I was an adolescent so I don't know what happened to the man that the boy must have grown up to be. Did he manage to retain his cheerful attitude or did life and its difficulties send him spinning into the mysterious, dark world where people retreat to, when the world becomes too much for them to handle? I wish I knew. Amma and I sometimes share our memories of the boy who brought so much sunshine into our lives just with his presence.

This book is dedicated to the memory of that boy. It is also written with the hope that reading this will somehow wake us all up to the many splendoured universe that we are born into, where each of us come packed with a unique gift. Not all of us will have the best IQ, the highest scores, or the stuff that 'successful' people have.

The people I met during the writing of *Gifted* taught me that it is possible to have a rainbow-coloured view of the world, even if you can't see. It is possible to run, jump with joy, and conquer the world, even if you can't use your legs. It is possible to wander in the wild and walk with tigers, even if you are not really able to walk. It is possible to paint a large canvas of possibilities for yourself, even if you don't have your arm. It is possible to listen and speak with your heart, even if you can't speak or hear. It is possible to give someone life, even if your own life has been spent on a wheelchair. It is possible to live the life of your dreams, even if the world sometimes thinks that you can't have a life at all…

Sudha Menon

'Siddharth is the bravest man I have met', said Dr Kiran Bedi after listening to his speech at the first India Inclusion Summit (IIS, 2012). Siddharth is a young man who was affected by cerebral palsy in his childhood but has overcome his disability to chart out an admirable life for himself. When I conceived the IIS during an informal chat with Dr Arun Shourie, I never dreamt of its impact at a societal level and the incredible people I would get to meet at a very personal level. In the years since I took the first fledgling steps to organize the summit, I have met many more Siddharths, each with a story of courage and indefatigable spirit. And each time I felt the same urgency to bring their stories out, so that the world does not forget them. Many of them participated, spoke, and performed at the IIS, got a brief mention in the media, and as always happens, were forgotten in a few days. For them, this book simply had to be written.

Having spent close to fifteen years in the corporate world, I have been studying 'leadership' and the qualities that make a good leader. Most leaders I know have become leaders because of a 'defining' moment in their lives—meeting an inspiring person, being in an accident, experiencing a traumatic moment or a tragedy that happened to a close family member or themselves, being born with a challenging health condition, or just witnessing a unique moment or situation. To my surprise, I noticed that each of the fifteen people in *Gifted* have the same traits that are displayed by leaders. To me, their stories are stories that will inspire each one of us. People who have jumped higher without limbs, seen without eyes, taught without speaking, moved people without moving, and above all, given hope to others and spread happiness around without expecting anything in return.

There are two kinds of responses to something terrible and traumatic: the same event can be profoundly damaging to one group while leaving the other better off for their experience. The special heroes of *Gifted* fall in the latter category. As author Malcolm Gladwell says in his book *David vs Goliath*, 'Not all difficulties are negative. Some are desirable!'

If leadership is about courage and the ability to overcome unsurmountable challenges, the stories of these individuals will be the best lesson.

This book would have remained as just one more wish in my growing list of ideas that never see the light of day, had it not been for my dear friend, Sudha Menon. When I told her about my idea and in particular about my inability to find time between my corporate life to pen down the stories of these 'special heroes', she jumped into the project, travelling relentlessly to meet and interview the heroes, and got down to the task of putting our book together. If writing is 1 per cent inspiration and 99 percent perspiration, Sudha has contributed to the 99 percent! This book has been our joint journey for two years and I can safely say that we have learnt more from the heroes of this book than from any leadership book or management college curriculum.

Right from the beginning of this project, we were clear of a few things. This book is not about us—the authors—but about the special heroes whose stories form the book.

India Inclusion Summit (IIS) 2013

'Ferose, I can't do this anymore', said Sridhar, my Executive Assistant, a week before the IIS-2013. Sridhar has been the pillar of the IIS, someone who has worked with me for a long time, someone with incredible passion and energy. I was aware of the long hours the team was spending—all beyond their regular office work—which in itself was demanding. For a moment, even I thought, *Have I created something so big that I can't handle it anymore?* The IIS takes almost a year to prepare. My entire staff and team of volunteers slog through the months before the event, working late hours and sacrificing their precious weekends, just to make it happen. During the last weeks before the event, I often ask myself why so many people are willing to spend their time doing this.

Hours after the IIS 2013 wrapped up, the core team came together for a traditional huddle to do a review of what went well and what didn't. I expected a complaint session from the team, given the exhausting time they had experienced. Instead, they surprised me with plans for the next year's event! Almost everyone was eager to start working on IIS-2014. People were so emotionally charged up that they had forgotten the long hours, the panic-stricken last-minute dash to make sure everything worked seamlessly, and the frustrating glitches that came out of nowhere. Sridhar proclaimed, 'It does not matter where I am or what I do, I sign up to run IIS for life!'. What energized the team was their undeniable contribution to creating a 'dent in the world'. This was their achievement.

One of the defining moments of the IIS 2013 was the performance of the Rajan brothers. They are gifted musicians who are visually challenged. While the audience was floored by the sheer singing talent of the brothers, what stood out for me was their mother, Snehalatha. During the performance, she stood behind her sons, proud to give them timely prompts to ensure a great performance. I have met Snehalatha multiple times after that and what inspires me is her positive spirit. I have always seen a smile on her face. Many of the stories in this book are about unsung heroes, especially the parents who probably suffer the most, because of perceived 'disabilities' of their children. This book is also a tribute to parents of individuals with disabilities—I bow in reverence to all of them!

When I met Virender Singh (a.k.a Goonga Pahalwan, the titular character of the documentary film with the same name about a deaf and mute wrestler's struggle to reach the Olympics), what moved me was the sheer simplicity of a man who has more medals than he can keep count of (According to Virender, he has 86 international medals and countless national ones!). He showed me the gold medals that he had won at the 2005 and 2013 Deaflympics, which he had kept wrapped up in a piece of paper! His only wish is to represent India in the

Olympics at Rio in 2016. The IIS is a platform to share the stories of unsung heroes like Virender and give them hope to fulfil that dream.

My personal story

It's 1 am and my son is burning up with 103 degrees fever. He has been crying non-stop for over an hour. The good news is, at least we know that he has fever so we can do something about it.

This is just one occasion. At other times, when he cries, we don't even know what's bothering him. Is it a stomach ache or a tooth ache? Is he hungry or thirsty? Or is it that he just does not like the position of the book that I have kept on the table? When you have a child who is non-verbal, you spend all your time trying to guess what is going on in his mind or what his needs are at any specific point. On most occasions it takes multiple attempts by me and my wife, Deepali, before we get it right and succeed in calming him down.

I just cancelled my 9 am flight so I can be with my son. I always book a cancellable ticket and I have stopped believing in the certainties of life!

Vivaan is 5 years old and he is on the Autism Spectrum.

Deepali once said to me, 'The day Vivaan calls me "mama", I am going to celebrate'. We have signed up for simple pleasures of life!

I have read every possible book on Autism. I have travelled across the world to meet Dr Temple Grandin, Prof Simon Baron Cohen, the late Dr Reeta Peshawaria, and Thorkil Sonne—all authorities in the field of Autism. While I have learnt a lot from all of them, my son has taught me a lot more—without uttering a single word!

This book is for him and the countless others—God's 'Special' children!

V. R. Ferose

Aisha Chaudhary

Aisha has used a phrase to describe her own journey—
'Singing in the life boat'. The art gives shape to that
phrase. The waves are swelling to swallow the boat
which is still sailing high and Aisha (the captain of the
boat) is depicted as a musical note. Its gentle curves
relate to the feminine personality and also with the
central theme of the phrase. All this is happening below
the gentle arc of the star-filled sky. The stars served as
guides to the ancient mariners in the open sea. The
stars are also those precious moments of happiness and
self-discovery in the reign of darkness.

It is not every day that an auditorium full of eminent people, mostly in their 40s who have carved their own niche in society, will listen with rapt attention when a teenager is delivering a speech. And it is possibly even rarer for them to then rise to their feet and applaud after that teenager has finished delivering the speech. But then, Aisha Chaudhry is no ordinary teenager and her speech, delivered at a high-profile TEDx event in Pune, where I was a fellow speaker, was on a subject that is otherwise associated with spiritual gurus, life coaches, and the philosophers: Being in the Present and Being Happy.

While the eighteen-minute TEDx talk was an eye-opener in itself, what made it even more compelling was the fact that the teenager who delivered it was actually on an oxygen tube that helped her breathe while she took on that task. Aisha Chaudhry's constant companion for the last few years has been a portable oxygen concentrator that she has been largely dependent on after she developed a debilitating condition called Pulmonary Fibrosis that reduced her lung function to just 20 percent of what it should have been.

Simply put, the spunky teenager has to struggle for every breath that she takes.

When she finished her talk that day, full of hope, courage,

and a belief that it will all fall into place one day, there was not a single eye in the auditorium that had not misted over or shed a tear.

Sometimes when I look back on the last three years of my life, I find it difficult to believe that I am living the life I am. I was such a shy teenager that I would drive everyone in the house crazy with my tears if I had to make a presentation in school. I did not want to be noticed or to talk in class if I could possibly avoid it but today my life is just the opposite. To me, it is unbelievable that I am now invited to prestigious events such as TEDx and that people are willing to spend their precious time listening to me speak about my journey towards finding happiness. I think it has to do with the fact that each of us has to struggle in life; what differentiates us is that our problems are different. But no matter what the nature of our problem or the extent of our struggle, all of us would like to get past our misery and find a life of happiness. I think my talks help them find that elusive happiness, not because I am giving them any big advice but because they believe that if I, with all my problems, can find happiness, then they too will be able to do that.

I am only 17, but I have possibly faced way more trials and challenges in life than other people my age. Even though I don't remember anything about it, my parents tell me that I was born with an immune deficiency disorder and that doctors told them I would not live beyond the age of 1. My parents refused to give up on me and shifted to the United Kingdom where I underwent a bone marrow transplant when I was a mere 6 months old. They were happy beyond measure when the transplant was a success but they did not know that fresh challenges waited around the corner for them. The condition left me very vulnerable to infection and this meant that for the first five years of my life, I had to largely live in isolation at home, without friends visiting me, because infection festers faster in closed spaces.

Little did my parents imagine that a side-effect of the transplant would rear its head in the form of pulmonary fibrosis, a condition that has left my lungs functioning at a mere 20 percent of their normal ability, when I entered my early teens.

Thankfully, I don't remember those early years of my life too much. What I remember is being a very fun-loving, happy kid. I was on steroids to keep a check on my health but I remember playing in the park with my mother and making a few friends, just like a normal kid. I remember the green dress I wore for my third birthday and I remember the first friend I ever made, and how happy I was that she was with me when we celebrated with a delicious chocolate cake.

My early years we spent in England and Holland and my life was fun despite my occasional ill health. As my health improved, I cycled in the park and made some friends with whom I became fairly close because we were in the same class at school for three years. We went on picnics to the beach and in Holland, I went to drama school and later put up plays for family and friends. I was a bold child and had no fear or inhibitions about putting myself out there and showing off my skills.

When I was about 12 or 13 years old, we moved back to

New Delhi, India, and that was hard because I faced a lot of bullying in middle school.

I am far more shy and withdrawn now from the years of being on my own during my adolescent years when I could never find acceptance from my classmates. I remained an outsider, the new girl from another country who could not do all the things that they could easily do: I couldn't run as fast as others, I couldn't walk as fast, I couldn't eat certain things, I didn't attend school as regularly as I should have, and I gradually withdrew into myself because of their jeers and taunts.

Once, on a school trip to Hrishikesh, I developed cold because of the chilly air in the mountains and because of my medical condition, I just could not stop coughing. My roommates were furious when their sleep was disturbed in the middle of the night and one of them told me to shut up or leave the room. I was sick and away from home, and I just didn't know what to do. Hurting from their rudeness, I ran straight to my nurse, crying. Because of my illness, the school required that I had to always travel with my nurse. That night, I was glad that she was with me and grateful for her kindness and understanding while I bawled my eyes out.

Middle school was definitely the worst time of my life. But it also made me grow as a person and made me much stronger. It made me realize that I have no control over how people react or behave and that I should not take it so personally. At that time, I was really sensitive and I was going through a lot, so I did let it break me, but I am no longer that person who was so vulnerable to external factors.

When I was 15 and going through a bad patch in life with

my health, something happened one day that changed my life. My dad came to me and told me about this talk that he had to deliver at an event on the subject: 'What Inspires Me'. My struggle to survive and my refusal to give up on life had inspired my dad to take up a project where they employ deaf and dumb people at Taco Bell and KFC, his workplace . He thought it would be easy for him to talk on what it is about me that inspires him but he said that when he got to writing down my journey, he found he was breaking down and was unable to talk about it at all! When the organizers heard his predicament and about me, they said it would be great if I, myself, could speak at that event. Dad was unsure because he knew I was shy but I even surprised myself when I said I would do it! I was not doing too much at school anyway because of my health issues. Besides, I had very few friends and I needed something to keep me busy. I felt the need to challenge myself and do something so that I would not mope so much about being homebound.

In retrospect, it was the best thing ever to happen in my life. I had no idea what to expect or what goes on at such events, and so I spent the next few weeks collecting ideas, quotes, and pictures, many from my own life. Since it was an event about inspiration and motivation, I decided to talk to the audience about the five things that my struggles had taught me. I called it 'Singing in the life boat' and it basically means that we can find things to celebrate even when we are in a shipwreck and in the middle of the ocean, on a life boat. I never knew then that this one thing would turn my life around and also make me introspect on how I would chart the rest of my own journey.

That new project consumed my life for an entire month. I rehearsed my talk in front of the mirror, in the car, and before going to sleep. I took videos of my talk and had fun doing it.

But walking onto the stage and delivering a speech with three hundred people in the audience was nerve-wracking. I was very nervous, worried I would make a mess of it even though I had taken cue cards of my speech. In the end, I managed to deliver it without any problem and was so proud when the audience got on their feet, applauding me. Suddenly, I wanted to do more of these talks. Maybe it was from the years of isolation or rejection, but I wanted to be with people and talking at events such as these was a perfect way of connecting with them. I was delighted when the organizers invited me to talk on the same subject at their next event at Jaipur.

I am often asked where I get the strength and a positive attitude to life despite the everyday challenges of my life, and I tell them that the way I live my life is a very deliberate choice.

In the last few years, my medical condition has exacerbated many times and I have found myself on a hospital bed, with tubes and needles all over my body. I have spent so many months homebound, unable to even sit up or turn in bed and often, I have worried myself thinking I would die from my illness. I have stayed up all night obsessing about my possible death till one day it occurred to me that death is a universal truth. We are all going to die one day, the only difference is that some of us will be gone sooner than others. And if that is the case, I should try to live my days happily instead of pitying myself.

Happiness is a choice we can make, an attitude we can adopt. I decided one day that instead of letting my illness and misery overwhelm me, I would find happiness in my everyday life. If I have to have pulmonary fibrosis (Pulmonary fibrosis is the formation or development of excess fibrous connective tissue in the lungs, also termed as 'scarring of the lung'), I choose to have a happy pulmonary fibrosis.

Once I made up my mind to be happy, I discovered joy in the small things in life. I have always wanted to paint and so I spend my days today painting the stuff that inspires me. My two dogs, Kobe, the Labrador and Rolo, the pug, are a constant source of happiness with their undying loyalty and their funny ways. Some of my best paintings are of them in their various moods, lolling on the bed with me, curled up in a corner snoozing, or bonding with each other. Dogs find happiness in the smallest things. They are delighted with a walk, excited with a small treat, and are in heaven when you tickle their bellies. There is a lot human beings can learn from them.

Over the years I have tried to convert my worst woes into an opportunity. Instead of feeling sad that I cannot go to school or study the subjects that my peers get to study, I have started using my time with the other things that fascinate me, such as trying my hand at modelling. I have always been fascinated at the idea that my photographs would be seen and appreciated by people I have never even met. My fascination with modelling gave me an opportunity once to get a full-fledged photoshoot done and all the while, I was seated on my wheel chair! That was incredibly exciting.

When my parents had to shift me to Mumbai for a few months last year so that I could escape the cold and the pollution in Delhi during the winter, I was saddened that I would miss school. But I realized that there was no real choice because my condition had exacerbated a few months back and I was at risk of further worsening of the situation if I did not move to the warmer climate of Mumbai. While I did miss the few friends I had, I decided to use my time after art classes to learn all about the art of applying makeup. It was as exciting as I imagined it to be and it never ceases to amaze me what can be achieved with a few deft strokes of a makeup brush and great colour. As part of the makeup course, I learnt not just tips for personal use but went backstage at a fashion show to see how artists use makeup for stage and screen. The other day I went backstage and watched as they put makeup on the actors who were putting up the play, *Grease*.

I have done other exciting things too, that I have stored away in a corner of my heart, such as taking off one day for a Broadway show in London, after a long day of painful and boring medicals tests and discussions about lung transplants at a hospital. I will always cherish that evening with my brother. I also remember walking down London's trendy Oxford Street with my mom, looking in at the stores, gaping at shop windows, and eating junk food, giggling like two friends out on a shopping date. Later, the family decided to go on a trip to Mauritius to rejuvenate after the endless hospital visits in London. It was fun even though I was sad I could not do the one thing that I wanted to do there: snorkel. I knew perfectly well that with my lungs in the condition they are, I could never dream of snorkelling but that did not stop me from wanting to do it. In the end, my family and I decided to get over the problem with the least danger to my health: I got into the snorkelling gear and dunked my head underwater for a single minute and in that tiny moment I saw so many vibrant, beautiful fish in the pristine blue waters. That moment, to me, meant everything.

Sometimes I think the hardships and struggles of life have made me a different person. When I was about 12, my health took a turn for the worse. I had become frail and underweight because I had no appetite and could barely eat. In the end, the doctors had to do a surgery in order to put a feeding tube in my stomach so that I would not be malnourished. It was the most painful thing I've experienced and I remember I was screaming in pain after I woke up after the surgery. In a way I think that surgery brought out memories of the other surgeries that I had when I was a small kid. While I screamed in pain for a long time, it also ended up being fun because I spent time with my mom at the hospital and we would stay up in bed watching *Grey's Anatomy*. We would crack jokes and the whole bed would shake from our combined laughter. It was fun as well as sad.

There have been times during my illness, especially a couple of years ago, when my condition trapped me in bed without even being able to turn over by myself, that I have been really confused and searched for answers about why I had to have this rare disorder. I have complained endlessly to my mother, cried and stormed to her about the unfairness of it, but through all of it, I have seen her being so strong and that has inspired me.

It's obviously hard to be strong all the time, but I have told myself I just have to try. That's all we can do.

When I start another bout of self-pity these days, I try and look beyond my own condition. For example, when I see homeless people living on the street, I feel blessed that I have a good home, a good family, my dogs, and I'm surrounded by such love. I look at the circumstances of those less fortunate than me and that's a powerful reminder to me to be grateful for what I have.

My talks at various events are a source of happiness. And so are my dogs: just playing with them and seeing the stupid things they do to get my attention is just so funny. I watch funny videos, do anything at all that keeps a smile on my face. Sometimes talking to someone who I haven't talked to in a while makes me very happy. I am not going to let my illness get the better of me.

Because I led a largely isolated life in my first five years, I couldn't be around people my age and that has made me awkward and a little shy. So I've always had very few friends, but now I have more friends, some from high school and some of them my brother's friends, and that makes me feel better. Most of them are in other parts of the world but because of the Internet we are able to connect sometimes, even though I feel sad I cannot see them face to face.

Now that I am close to finishing my diploma in Arts, I dream of other things that I could do. I've always wanted to go to the Arts University in Bournemouth, England. They can tailor-make courses for people with special needs and have really good facilities for the differently-abled, so I thought that would be a good place to go.

I love to travel and the one thing about my illness that I am really sad about is that I can't travel too much. I want very badly to fly to America and my dream is to go to Spain and explore the famed beauty of that country. But these dreams will probably never come true because high altitudes make my oxygen rate go very low, and I have to have oxygen on board the flight.

There are the other daily things which I go through that are sometimes very annoying. There are the regular coughing fits in the morning and night that get to the point where I can't breathe, and there's nothing really I can do but have my medicines and get on the oxygen machine. I have to sleep with it all the time.

Sometimes it annoys me that I am tied to a machine and a person at all times. Everyone stares at me and pities me, and that's not what a teenager wants. I hate that I'm not able to do a lot of things like being able to go out alone, travel, to breathe, to just be normal. So in that sense I really don't have a normal 17-year-old girl's life.

But every day I reiterate to myself that the important thing is to live in the moment. I often tell myself that to spend even a moment crying and cursing my life is a waste because I am never going to get that one moment back.

It is, of course, easier said than done because the hardships from the illness are very overpowering. Sometimes I feel like I'm swallowed up by them. But I'm trying to be bigger than my illness.

I bless my stars that I have a really good relationship with my parents. Ours is not a normal parent-child relationship. Instead, they're like my friends because I spend the most time with them. I can express myself freely to them without the fear of being chided. I enjoy being with them and I have learnt a lot from them, including how to keep relationships strong and intact. My mom always says that many couples get divorced because of the pressures that a sick child puts on their relationship. But my parents have been very strong as a couple throughout my illness. After my transplant, my mom and I had to live in the UK for three years and my dad had to be in India so that my brother could continue with his schooling. Dad was also busy with work so we were separated as a family for a few years. But instead of drifting apart, the distance pulled us closer.

My parents have been my best teachers, too. I've learnt strength from my mother and from my dad, I have learnt to forgive, forget, and to be loyal. When I get really frustrated with my friends for betraying me or talking behind my back, he always tells me to forgive and forget. He's shown me, with his own friends, that you can do that and it makes you a better person. I've learnt about relationships from him and how to put ourselves in another person's shoes so we can understand exactly what they are going through. He inspires me with the way he treats people with such love that each one feels special. Surrounded by so much love, the onus is on me to try and be happy and make others happy too.

I believe in miracles now and dare to dream of a normal life for myself. Maybe my fibrosis will go away and then I will get all that I dream of: a job and a family of my own….. Till then I am determined to make the most of this wonderful gift of life that God has given me. As writer Hans Christian Anderson once said, 'Enjoy life, there's plenty of time to be dead.'

Ankit Jindal

Ankit has been depicted as a graph, with a white and bold line-chart that stands out as a stark contrast from the black background. The motif of a graph relates to Ankit in more ways than one. A graph is a common motif in the world of business and management, the profession he belongs to. Also the cardinal points of the graph pin the low and high points of his own journey, and yet its upward rising trend beams out the success he has carved out of his life. The black background, in some ways, is the darkness at a physical level and the white lines of the chart is his counter-attack to conquer his disability with sheer will and determination.

Ankit was a fun-loving teenager of 13 when a routine eye check-up at school, followed by a visit to the ophthalmologist, brought his world crashing down around him. The doctors were categorical in their verdict: he was suffering from retinitis pigmentosa, a progressive disorder where the patient gradually loses his vision. Ankit was no stranger to the world of the visually impaired. The genetic disorder was passed down to him from his maternal side—his grandfather, four aunts, and an uncle all had it. The disease advanced rapidly and in just under twelve years after the diagnosis, Ankit had lost 90 percent of his vision. The happy-go-lucky boy who played cricket with his cronies found himself first reading his lessons in large font, then using a magnifying glass, and eventually giving up reading when he found he could not even read bold headlines in newspapers with the help of high-powered glasses.

'At the age of 13, when most teenagers have dreams and start making plans for their future, I was faced with the harsh reality that I would soon be blind and would have to spend the rest of my life in darkness, dependent on somebody for my everyday needs. It was a scary truth but I knew that to give in to my anxiety and to give up was not an option. My parents were shattered when they heard the diagnosis but I had grown up seeing my aunts and uncle live a normal life despite their limited vision. I decided I, too, would live the life that I wanted, without letting my visual impairment pull me down. I told myself I would not quit the game. But somewhere at the back of my mind I also knew that mere acceptance was not going to be enough. I knew I would have to stay focused and be positive through my life because it would be a fight for survival.

'I am glad I did not give up because if I had, I would have lost out on all the exciting things that I have done with my life in the last few years,' the 28-year-old told me, sitting at the coffee shop in the sprawling campus of IT major, Wipro last year. Listening to his story and the experiences that have shaped him these last fifteen years since he lost his vision, I could not agree more.

As a child, when I would play cricket with my friends outside our home in Mumbai, my bat would often miss the ball when I went in for a shot. That, and my constant habit of squinting, was a joke among my friends but one day, that joke turned serious when, after a series of visits to doctors, it became clear that I, too, had the genetic disorder that had left my maternal grandfather, aunts, and an uncle blind.

It was difficult to accept at first that I would have to spend my life in darkness and as a dependent, but gradually I made peace with the fact. I started adjusting to living with reduced vision, using large fonts, a magnifying glass, high-powered glasses and eventually, my mother, Sarla Jindal, as a reader/helper for my studies. I was among the toppers in class and had no intention of letting my poor vision affect that status! I first started using a magnifying glass during 10th grade but by the end of my graduation, I could not read books on my own. At the age of 19 or 20, I was completely dependent on others. It was not easy at all to come to terms with but I was determined not to give up.

During my graduation years, I managed by paying a little extra attention during the classes. I believed in the importance of practical learning, so I would also participate in a lot of competitions unlike my friends who spent time only with their books. I did my graduation in Business Management at Surana College in Bengaluru, which held a variety of competitions across all streams, such as a 'business plan' competition that involved creating a financial model and analyzing it at various stages etc. I learnt a lot from taking part in such competitions.

My mother would sit with me and help out, even though she was not equipped to handle complex financial matters. Her courage was immeasurable, especially if you consider that a few years after my diagnosis, my younger brother, Pratik, too, was diagnosed with the same disorder and started losing his sight rapidly. She was an ordinary homemaker but she has played an extraordinary role in shaping the lives of her two sons. More than any other external help, we depended on her for our studies and for navigating through our newly-dark lives. Thankfully for me, my vision lasted till I was into my second year of my graduation and so, I was able to write my own examination papers. I did not know then that in the years to come, the search for a scribe to help me finish the rest of my education would be a challenging, frustrating task.

Almost immediately after I cleared my 10th grade exams, various members of my large Marwari business family started hinting that I should join the garments business that my father, Rajiv Jindal, owned. They were well-meaning people and possibly thought that it was better for a blind boy to be in the security of the family business rather than struggle elsewhere. But I had other plans for myself. My father was clear in his message to me and my brother that we could study as long as we wanted to.

In 2002, we moved to Bengaluru. My father had suffered a

setback in his business and we were not very well-off financially. I signed up for a Bachelor of Business Management course and sailed through it, possibly because business acumen comes naturally to those born into business families. Also, I listened keenly to programming on CNBC and honed my understanding of the things happening in the business world.

It was when companies arrived at our college campus for placements that I first started realizing how skewed the world is against people with disabilities. I was interviewed by many and rejected because I was blind. Then, one of India's top three software service providers arrived at the campus and unlike others, when I asked them if they were open to employing a blind person, they advised me to apply, assuring me that they would look at my case like they did other candidates', too.

This company had an external consultant, Rama Chari, who was helping them hire people with disability in order to make the organization more inclusive and that proved providential for me because she ensured that the training was made inclusive, and the trainers were sensitized to the issue of disability.

All the graduates who were hired were put into a big pool and had to undergo a training process after which everyone was given a responsibility. Unfortunately, I did not get a responsibility right away.

During my holidays, I had come to know about JAWS (Job Access with Speech), a software that reads all screen content including installation instructions and key commands aloud so that visually impaired users can start programmes, read documents, and surf the web with the help of just their keyboards. I got this software, which has revolutionized life for people with visual impairment, a month before joining my employer, and it proved timely for me. Getting through the first few days at the new job was a formidable task. A computer skills test required recruits to have a speed of at least 30 words per minute with 80 percent accuracy. On day one, my speed was 4 words per minute with 20 percent accuracy and I was told clearly that I had twenty days in which to either shape up or ship out. That was when I almost stopped sleeping during the nights when I would pound away at my computer till my fingers threatened to drop off. On the 22nd day, when the test was conducted, I scored 29 words per minute with 100 percent accuracy. My trainer had tears in her eyes and was proud that I had proved my ability categorically.

At every point in my life in the last ten years or more, technology has played a crucial role in enabling me. So while the computer helped me become productive at work, or made me employable, my iPhone has helped me really become far more efficient in my day-to-day activities. For instance, I use Google maps anywhere I go. I direct my driver instead of being dependent on him. I do all of my banking on my phone today. I do all my reading—*Harvard Business Review*, business, self-help books, and even Paulo Coelho—on my phone. I wish I had this technology during my graduation or my MBA days.

In the initial six months at my first job, no manager was ready to take me in. There were a few other visually impaired people, but they were always in a support function in the company's BPO. Rama Chari, the consultant who was advising the company on disability issues, was keen that I should enter a business role at the company. It was a period of highs and lows but I knew it was important for me to hang on. I knew I could do a lot more than people perceived me to be capable of but for six months, when I had no work at the company, I sat in the cafeteria/ pantry area, volunteering my services for some of the initiatives the Human Resources department were doing.

As it turned out, my volunteer work became an opportunity for me to showcase my ability. It began with me developing a questionnaire for HR to gauge the employee satisfaction levels of people with disability who worked in the organization. It was my first assignment and I created the report, analyzing it before I showcased it to the HR department. Luckily for me, that report went right up to the VP, HR level. Rama would make sure that my seniors knew I had done it, so it strengthened my chances to get a role at work. She was the one who taught me to be patient, saying that given some time, one or the other department would surely take me in. She wanted to prove that people with visual impairment could also do the same work that normally-abled people can, given the right support and work environment.

My first big break came when a manager gave me a role which was called 'no call, no show' which basically, is all about calling up absconding employees who just stop coming to work one fine day without giving notice. My role was to get in touch with them and get them back to work. The organization's expectation was that I should manage to get at least 10–12 percent of the errant employees back. So if I was able to get 10 out of the 100 people who had left back to work for the company, they'd be very happy. The person who was doing it before me managed to get back 8-9 per 100.

I realized right away that speed wasn't as important here as empathy and other intuitive skills that would get through to the missing employees. It was a jackpot when I managed to touch the 30 percent level, completely impressing my seniors. At that point, BPO companies were suffering from very high attrition rates and to be able to bring 30 percent of the employees back into the fold was a great achievement. I worked the telephone continuously, and there were cases where I had to step in and talk to parents, sometimes spouses, and other stakeholders, before I could get the employee back.

My reports on this particular process created news within the company because in many cases it exposed insensitive managers who would be responsible for significant attrition. The reports would go to the HR department of all our businesses and what started out as a quarterly report soon became a monthly and later, a weekly report. Suddenly, people wanted to know the reasons why employees left their jobs and they also wanted to know how they could stem the tide. Since I was getting 30 out of the 100 absconding employees back, it was like having an impact of 30 percent to the organization's bottom line, in various ways. The company did not have to hire additional people as stand by, nor did they have to spend time and money training them, and they did not lose business continuity because of the sudden exit of employees.

My success boosted my confidence a lot because now I was contributing meaningfully to the organization. It also resulted in me being made part of the management council for attrition at the company. I did not realize at that point how significant a development that was but when I reflect upon it now, it was a huge thing for a new recruit to be part of such a critical process. Later, I was also part of several workshops on the same subject and that added to my standing within the organization.

Sometime in 2007, I collaborated with Rama Chari and two others—Sakshi Broota, Rama's colleague at the National Centre for Promotion of Employment for Disabled Persons (NCPEDP), and Vijay Krishnamani, a colleague of mine with hearing impairment—to set up a social enterprise, Diversity and Equal Opportunity Centre (DEOC), dedicated to making workplaces more inclusive. As a person with disability, I had experienced all the frustration, the cynicism, and the discrimination that is accorded to all of us and I knew exactly what changes needed to be made to make it a better world for us. Because I was blessed with a supportive family and a few friends, my journey had been relatively smooth but I knew that that was not the case for the majority of people with disability. I wanted to give back to the society which had hand-held me during my worst times and setting up DEOC with a few like-minded people was a great way of doing it. We decided we would be the bridge between corporate houses, NGOs in the disability space, and advocacy groups working on issues relating to people with disability. The next few years were emotionally a very satisfying phase of my life as DEOC grew into an organization that consulted companies developing strategy for promoting inclusion, writing, and reviewing policies on equal opportunity, conducting accessibility audits for them, and training them.

One of our first projects was Project Communicate, where we tied up with IT services company, Mphasis. We said to them that we would get some forty people with disabilities from smaller towns around Bengaluru and make them employable with a two-month residential training module. At the end of the sixty days, 38 of the 40 people we had trained got employed as Business Process Executives, while the remaining two dropped out on their own. After training three more batches of people with disabilities, we shifted our focus to training the trainers, skilling up a number of NGOs who work in the disability space. We organized a 'Train the Trainer' programme with the support of Mphasis and handed over the training module to NGOs to take it forward.

Meanwhile, DEOC realized the information gap that existed about disability employment—not just with companies but also among NGOs. In 2007, DEOC also started work on a project with the Confederation of Indian Industries, an initiative that would make corporate India more aware and sensitive about inclusion at workplaces. Being co-author for *Values Route to Business Success: The Why and How of Employing Persons with Disabilities*, the country's first ever handbook on the entire cycle of hiring people with disabilities, will remain a cherished part of my own journey. It was two years of hard work, coordinating and consulting with over a dozen experts/ institutions working in this space, but was time and effort well spent because that book is now the single point of reference for anybody wanting to hire people with disabilities.

Meanwhile, at the company where I worked, I soon became a Subject Matter Expert, one of the fastest promotions for a newcomer in the company. By the time I decided to leave the company to do my Masters in Business Management, I was managing a 15-member team that encompassed all twenty backend processes of an employee's life cycle at the BPO.

An MBA was not what I dreamt of when I was a kid. As an adolescent, I dreamt of becoming a chef. The time I spent in the kitchen baking cakes, churning up ice creams or exotic sandwiches were happy times and they also made me popular in my extended family. But it was not an ambition that found approval in the business family that I was born into. My uncle said to me once, 'You are a businessman's son and you want to become a cook?' So I put my dreams of becoming a chef behind me and decided I would focus on getting an MBA.

I was determined to do an MBA from a reputed college and after two attempts when I did not make the cut due to my work commitments, I was a little despondent. In 2007, my younger brother got through his MBA entrance test after he finished his engineering course and that proved to be a catalyst for me to work harder. A cousin of mine, Diwakar Gupta, who had shifted to Bengaluru, convinced me to focus on clearing my entrance, saying that I had an entire lifetime to prove myself at my workplace but I had to get on with my dream of getting my MBA. It was a very difficult year because I had just been promoted at work and had to prove myself worthy of that. My father was bed-ridden with slip-disk and mom had to attend to him during the day and sit up with me at night to read my lessons to me. It was a difficult journey for both of us because we had to steal time from other important commitments. I had my frustrations with my scribes also during those times because different institutions interpreted the qualifying criteria for a scribe differently and changed them without notice. It was financially and emotionally draining to keep changing scribes.

At the Faculty of Management Studies, Delhi, from where I eventually did my MBA, my subjects were Strategy, HR, and Marketing. The stay in Delhi, living alone for the first time ever and navigating my way through unknown places, was life altering. It was a very unfamiliar city and having to navigate it independently was challenging, as was keeping my room in shape and doing my studies with discipline. It was also difficult to get past the unhelpful stance of the teachers. One particular professor once said to me that he did not understand why people like me (blind) wanted to do an MBA. It was a very hurtful thing to say to someone who had consistently done well in academics. I was rated as the best employee at work, I was among the toppers in college, and had got admission into the MBA course on merit.

Writing the entrance exam for the MBA course itself was a nightmare when I realized that they had given me a scribe who had studied in the regional language in Karnataka and was not proficient in English. It was only because I was aware of my rights as a person with disabilities that I finally managed to get a more qualified scribe for myself.

My early days at the management school were traumatic. It was highly competitive and the course was very intensive so nobody could really find the time to handhold me. When campus summer placement time came along in the first year, my work experience and my very obvious good performance impressed nobody. One particular consulting firm conducted three rounds of interviews and I was slotted to get placed but for one of their senior leaders who said they could not possibly hire a person with disability! I was shattered. Eventually I was placed at a company floated by an alumni of the school and I felt it was more his generosity than the fact that I was qualified for a good job! My confidence hit an all-time low at that point and I struggled to find my moorings.

It was a long, hard journey back on my feet, something I pulled off by calling on all my reserves and jumping into all kinds of competitions that the college held. It was difficult to find partners because nobody wanted a blind person as a partner. What clinched the deal for me was when I led a team that became the first runner-up for the prestigious Tata Business Leadership Awards, with a business plan for e-waste management for Tata group companies. I had finally claimed my place in the college and there was no looking back after that.

Our work with DEOC seemed far more crucial to me after I went through fresh trauma during the final placements after my MBA. It was a season of disappointments before Wipro came to our campus. Then, happily for me, getting placed was an easy thing for me because Wipro is an inclusive organization which did not look at my disability as much as they looked at my ability. I've been working as a Marketing Manager for Wipro Infotech and Global Infrastructure Services for three years now.

At Wipro my very first manager, Sarika Naik, could spot my strengths immediately and gave me work that I could deliver. Wipro is an extremely inclusive organization that goes the extra mile to understand the needs of people with disabilities. At various points people have had queries about my abilities but I have always let my work talk for me. I have never let cynicism or the judgement of other people affect my work or my life.

My desire to work in the disabilities sector continued

unabated. An exploratory meeting with Vidhya Ramasubban, an activist for inclusion and the rights of people with disabilities, led to my getting involved in the setting up of yet another social enterprise, Wheels of Change, that started the country's first inclusive cab service for people with disabilities. It was a fascinating concept for me because I myself have faced several difficulties while commuting. When we launched KickStart Cabs in September 2013, it was in response to a crying need for transportation for this segment and it is possibly the country's first inclusive cab service for persons with disabilities. The company offers customized cars with removable seats or seats that actually can come out of the car at the push of a button and double up as a wheel chair. Raised roofs and other customizations allow ease of entry for users. In addition, drivers are trained to assist users in every way—they will escort a visually impaired person inside their destination, communicate with hearing impaired customers through SMS, and are sensitive to the needs of this segment.

In December 2013, I was overjoyed when I was chosen as one of the role models among people with disability for the 15th Helen Keller Awards given by the NCPEDP. It was my reward for my own determination to never give in to my circumstances. I had vowed to myself at 13 that I would make my parents proud and later that I would help the cause of people like me. Walking up the stage with my father to collect that award from the hands of Kumari Selja—then Union Minister of Social Justice & Empowerment of India—was one of the happiest moments of my life.

It was also a happy moment for my wife Kanika, the young

girl who refused to back down from her determination to marry me. Her parents were not happy that she wanted to marry a person with disability and tried their best to dissuade her. I remember I first spoke to her over the phone, after some relative told my parents about this prospective bride. By then I was so tired of the rejection by potential brides and their parents—nobody wants a blind husband or son-in-law—that I told this new girl right away that I was blind. My parents had warned me that if I continued to do this, I would end up remaining single but I was surprised when Kanika did not mind that at all.

Even today I find it hard to believe that when her parents refused to relent, she stood up to them, saying she would go ahead with the wedding even without their blessings. It is a tough thing for a girl from a Punjabi family to pull off and it increased my admiration for her. The marriage eventually happened and I took my in-laws to the ceremony when I got the Hellen Keller award and they finally realized that it does not matter that I am blind. What matters is the substance within a human being, his spirit, and his ability to get over obstacles.

I have never let my visual impairment stop me from doing the things I have wanted to do. I'm an adventure sports enthusiast and have done everything from white-water rafting in Nepal and Rishikesh to cliff jumping and mountain trekking.

I want the world to know that having a disability does not mean that we cannot have dreams of our own. Someday, I want to become the CEO of a company and also want to continue with my work in the social sphere to take up projects that add value to the life of people with disability.

Ashwin Karlik

The window shows important touch points in Ashwin's life—an engineering degree, a job in a software company, tryst with the greatest cricketer—and this window has two flaps, and they are analogous to Ashwin and Bharat. All those things we see in between are their shared dreams and their realities. The window is incomplete without each of them and so are their lives. Both the flaps together have opened up the window of possibilities.

You wake up one day and something life-altering happens to you. It comes upon you unbidden, but when you experience it, something inexplicable, something you can't define happens inside, and you are not the same person anymore. Meeting with Ashwin Karthik and his life-long pal Bharat Sharma, was one of those moments for me.

On a mild winter Bengaluru morning, when the frenzy of office-goers and the impatient honking of cars had not yet commenced, I made my way to Koshy's—the iconic hangout off IT city's busy MG Road.

I was a bit worried. Would I be able to handle this interview without any major faux pas, without hurting anyone's sentiment? Like most of us, I have spent the better part of life without coming into any major contact with people with disability and meetings with the few people I have come into contact with have been fleeting. And now I was about to meet a young man, a software engineer who is also a quadriplegic, and I just did not know what to expect. Would he be on a wheel chair? Did he walk at all? How would I greet him? Could I shake hands with him?

All those fears went out of the window the moment I set my eyes on the charming young man who greeted me with a thousand watt smile from inside the car where he waited patiently for me to arrive. Ashwin's companion on the car drive, a well-built young man, opened the door and gently, much like a mother would do, lifted him of the seat and put him on the ground. 'Good to meet you, ma'am,' Ashwin said, bestowing his dazzling smile upon me once again as we made our way inside the hotel, Bharat patiently guiding him to a table across the room and seating him, unmindful of the curious glances of the wait staff and the couple of others who are in for early breakfast.

I have heard about their extraordinary friendship, read about it in disbelief, but seeing is believing and the for the next couple of hours I listened and watched as Ashwin told me his amazing story of grit and determination, of making a life for himself aided by Bharat who put his life on hold and devoted four years of his time to be his friend's scribe as he wrote his engineering college exams. I grappled with trying to understand their equation—at times, they were like two best friends on a shared journey but when Bharat fed him a vegetable cutlet patiently, piece by piece, and wiped off an errant stream of coffee trickling down Ashwin's chin, he became a fond mother tending to her child.

They laugh together, fight with each other, go to music concerts and cricket matches, and never, ever, eat ice-cream without each other. As I listened to the saga of one man's fight to survive against all odds to follow his dreams and the other's dogged determination to make his friend's dreams come true, the cups of tea on the table lay forgotten.

When I left a few hours later, my spirit was immensely uplifted from watching the two and their boundless affection. In an increasingly materialistic world where each of us is on a self-seeking mission, where there is no time to stand and stare, leave alone spend a lifetime in the service of a fellow human being, my meeting with Ashwin and Bharat helped re-instill my hope in human kind.

When I was a born, the doctor told my mother that her baby was a cerebral palsy—quadriplegic—the motor function in all four of my limbs were affected and that I would never be anything more than a doll. 'Take him home but don't expect anything out of him because you will be disappointed,' the doctor told her.

My mother narrated this incident to me a long time ago and also told me how she responded to the doctor's comment. She said that she decided at that moment that no matter how much it took out of her and my father, she would make sure that I made something out of my life. She probably never imagined whan an uphill task it would be, but she decided she would devote her entire life to proving that no matter what medicine says, there is nothing that a determined human being can't do, with will power, hard work, and love.

Sometimes when I look back, I find it hard to believe that I am a software engineer today, working with one of India's best-known Information Technology companies. I never imagined I would be the first cerebral palsy quadriplegic to become a BE graduate in India. Each day, I marvel at the fact that I have been working with Mphasis's testing division for seven years now and that I am a valued member of their off-shore delivery team.

I would never have thought that I, with all my problems,

could one day get the NCPEDP Shell-Helen Keller award for 2011.

The life I am living today is very removed from where I began in life. Even though I had the complete support and endless love of my parents and my brother, it was a tough life. School was a challenge because I could not keep pace with the rest of the class, but my mother was not about to allow that to keep me from being one of the toppers in class. She and I sat up at night and she went over my lessons with me till I had mastered them. I had an unquenchable thirst for learning even back then and I remember some days she would fall asleep while helping me with a subject but I would refuse to let her sleep till I had finished my lessons!

If my mother is the pillar of my life, the one who believes that I can achieve what a normally-abled person can achieve, my father was my hero, the person who discussed cricket with me and encouraged me to keep writing, when I first started writing poetry. He was interested in everything I did and kept me involved in dozens of things at all times. He passed away when I was still a teenager, leaving me shattered. I felt there was no one anymore to share my writing with and so, I stopped writing poetry—till one day I met Bharat, my friend who is today the first to read every word that I write. Bharat was the son of one of my father's friends but initially, we were not close to each other because he thought I was a geek and a nerd while he was a keen sportsperson.

My love for studies continued and each time I came out as one of the toppers in class, my confidence in myself grew, but when my 10th grade exams came along, I was in a quandary. I was sure I would not finish writing the paper on time because my condition makes my writing very slow. Despite that, when the results came along, I was very happy when I scored 84 percent marks. My 12th grade exams were a wakeup call. My performance suffered hugely because I was not able to find the right scribe and I ended up with 70 percent marks while I had never scored below 90 percent in any exam previously. I was so upset with this that I insisted on writing my first year engineering exam myself, with twenty minutes extra writing time that the college allowed me. It was a complete disaster because I could not even get around to addressing half the questions and I ended up flunking three papers. In the depths of misery, I decided to quit my engineering course and pursue a BSc degree instead but Bharat and mom would have none of it.

It was Bharat who stepped in at this time and changed my life. He had taken a year off after his 12th grade so that he could study hard to make the cut for the centralized exams for admission to the engineering course. When he realized I was in a quandary, he decided to put his own academic ambitions on hold so that I could fulfil mine. Part of the reason why he had to do this was because the scribe allowed for engineering college students are required to be studying in the 12th grade or lesser and that makes it very difficult because most 12th graders are busy with their own studies and won't volunteer to be a scribe for anybody.

I never imagined that Bharat's helping hand would culminate in his being my scribe till I finished my engineering degree, being one of the toppers in the final semester with 83 percent marks. Those who know our story know that Bharat had a tough time when he initially decided to take a break from studies and devote himself to me till I had become an engineer. His father stopped talking to him and there was a time when he was not welcome at his home anymore, which was understandable because he was the eldest son in the family and they feared he was throwing his life away for someone else.

As difficult as it is to imagine now, I spent the two years after my engineering degree locked up at home in Bengaluru where we had shifted. My mom and brother had to go to work in the day and they were afraid to leave me alone in the house, so they thought it better to lock me inside. Nobody wanted to hire a disabled engineer. Bharat would keep taking me to various IT company campuses where I would crack all the interview rounds. Then they would ask me to prove to them that I was capable of walking independently and questioned me how I would cope with eight-hour shifts and how I would manage to visit the toilet by myself. The level of cynicism and lack of belief in the ability of those with disability is shocking. I would get angry and tell them that I had the qualifications, I had proved myself, and how I managed in the toilet was not their problem at all. But that never got me a job.

It was then that Bharat took me to a software testing course my sister-in-law had found for me, which I completed. But my misadventures with finding a job continued. At many places, they would ask me to demonstrate my typing skills and when I typed with the only functioning finger on my right hand, they would say, 'You can type better and faster if you use both your hands!' Often, I would be in a rage and ask them if they could not see that I could not possibly use both my hands. Often, I would descend into deep bouts of depression after these interviews.

It was my brother who finally found a small start-up company where they said I could hang around and learn by observing was happening there. I was not paid to help out but I was glad just to be given the opportunity for me to do something other than staying cooped up at home. They were even kind enough to say that if I did learn something, they could possibly hire me in the future to train new recruits.

It was around that time that the then Chief Minister of Karnataka, Mr Kumar Swamy, started organizing a Janata Darshan project where he met common citizens directly to understand their problems. One morning, out of the blue, Bharat called to say that he had spent the entire night standing in queue outside the venue of the darbar so that we could go and meet the CM and tell him about my plight. Bharat said I was to join him along with mom and my brother.

We got there and Bharat had just three minutes to tell Mr Swamy why he was there, so he quickly told him I was an engineer who no one wanted to employ because of my disability. Mr Swamy referred us to the Social Welfare Minister who we met the next day and that was the turning point of my life. The minister immediately guided us to Enable India where we met Vidya, a wonderful woman who is herself blind but works with disabled people. The next day, we were at their office in Bengaluru and it was a new experience for them as well as me. Shanti Raghavan, the lady who runs Enable India, said that I was very different from the other physically challenged people who approached the organization because while a large number of them had studied only till 12th grade, I was an engineer. As usual, Bharat was my scribe for the aptitude test that they took and I cleared that very well. Almost immediately after that, I went for the first interview with Mphasis, and I must confess I went with little hope because of my past rejections. Which is why, when the company offered me a job that very day, I was so surprised that I did not even notice that the offer letter said 'Ashiwini' instead of 'Ashwin'! In fact, I had to pinch myself many times to believe that I finally had a job. I had lost all hope of ever getting a job and was waiting for Bharat to finish his studies so that he could help me write my Masters in Technology exams, but all of that changed when I held that offer letter in my hand. When I called up my brother at work, he realized I had found myself a job, simply by the joy and excitement in my voice. When I reached home that evening, all our friends were waiting to congratulate me and celebrate my big day. My mother was in tears almost the entire time, unable to believe that our struggles had finally paid off.

When the company informed me that I would have to go to Mangalore for a three-month training period, we were worried. Bharat was in college, mom was working, my brother was working abroad, and I had never been anywhere on my own. I need not have worried though, because Bharat accompanied me there for a week, fibbing to his college authorities that he was ill. My mother later took over from me for the rest of my stay. Thankfully, the stint at Mangalore was not at all difficult because as soon as they realized that a disabled person was visiting, the management put up temporary ramps so that the campus was accessible for me!

I remember my first salary was Rs 10,000 and I went for a movie with all the friends I made at the campus. Now that I was an earning member of the family, I decided that I wanted to buy a gift for mom so one day, with a friend from my company, I arrived at the market in Mangalore to buy her a saree. It took us hours to get the project done because I had never stepped into a saree shop before and had no clue about either the cost or the kind of saree mom would like. In the end, the kind saleswoman at the counter helped me. When I walked into the house with the red satin saree I had purchased for her, there were tears in my mom's eyes. I don't think she liked the saree much because it was too bright but she wore it happily and proudly because her son, who was never expected to do anything in life, had bought it for her with his salary.

It has been nearly seven years now since I joined Mphasis and each day, I have gained confidence in myself and in my own abilities. There have been many ups and downs in my life but I am in a happy place now.

When I look back today, one of the most fulfilling moments of life was the time I got to touch my certificate of graduation. I was the boy who was jeered by his classmates, the guy who could never become a graduate because I would never do the drawings required for the course, and yet, here I was, topping the class with 83 percent marks. I kept asking mom and Bharat if that was really my name on the certificate and they said I had earned it by working doubly hard. My brother and sister-in-law were abroad at that point and those were the days when there were no mobile phones. Bharat went out and made an international call to my brother conveying the news of my graduation and they immediately called us back. There was hardly any conversation during that phone call because we were all crying with joy!

I will never forget the kindness of the people who helped me chase my dreams and make them happen. If it were not for my mother and Bharat, and their belief in me, I would not be where I am today. When my father died, mom took up a job so that she could raise her two children. She had always been a homemaker but after his death, she had to play the dual role of a devoted mother and a committed professional. My life would not be the same but for Bharat. Not many will give up even a minute of their time for the somebody else but Bharat kept his studies aside for four years after his 12th grade exams and became my shadow in that period in the little town of Chikmaglur that we lived in. He would take me to my class during my first year engineering and stand outside the class all day, taking down copious notes because I was not able to take down notes myself. When I was miserable because I could not take on the job of engineering drawings, my lecturer stepped in and took me under his wings, giving me his time till I understood the concept clearly. And once I had learnt how to do the drawings, he taught me how to teach Bharat to make those drawings so that he could do the same while being my scribe during exams. I remember so many nights I would keep Bharat awake well past midnight till he was able to deliver the drawings exactly as I had envisaged it in my head!

My life has been full of ups and downs but somewhere along the way, I have learnt to deal with the downs with equanimity. Not everybody will be appreciative of who you are and what you can do, but I have learnt to not get myself worked up when someone talks negatively about me at work. I simply let my work do that talking for me.

In December last year, I was chosen for the National Best Employee Award given by the Ministry of Social Justice and it was something that I would never have imagined even in my wildest dreams. When I received that award from the President of India at Vighyan Bhavan, it was almost unreal for me. My mother, of course, was unbelievably happy and Bharat told me later that when I got that award, he felt like he himself had achieved something in life.

A few years ago when Rotary Midtown and the Brigade group selected me for their Young Achiever Award, they also made it a moment of shared joy and pride for us by giving Bharat a special prize—Friend in a Million—to him, for being a source of inspiration to others. They were impressed with his selfless devotion to me and by his steadfast belief in my abilities. He had put his life on hold so that I could achieve my dreams and our shared journey had inspired them enough to make it an example for others to follow.

Four years ago, Bharat gave me one of the most treasured gifts of my life—a meeting with my hero, Sachin Tendulkar, when he was in Bengaluru to play an IPL match against the Royal Challengers. At the function where we were given the Rotary-Brigade group awards, we had struck up a friendship with cricketer Robin Uthapa. One day, Bharat told me we were to meet Robin and his friends at the hotel where the cricket teams were staying. After hanging around making small talk, Robin said we should head to his friend's room but when we got there the nameplate on the door said Sachin Tendulkar. I was left speechless when we knocked and Sachin himself opened the door to welcome us saying he had been waiting to meet me since the night before, after he heard my story from Robin. And when he hugged me and made me sit beside him, I could not believe it was happening. I was sitting in the same room as the man I had wanted to meet ever since I was a child. My father had promised me that he would one day help me meet my hero but when he passed away, I had given up on that dream. Even today I can't believe that we spend over an hour chatting and watching Formula One with him and taking pictures. When we left, he gifted me a t-shirt and asked me if I would be his friend. I will never forget that moment. Sachin has been a great friend ever since then. He is one of the most sincere and committed people I have met. Every year, no matter where he is in the world, he calls to wish me 'Happy Birthday' and that never fails to make my day!

From Sachin, I learnt to not be shy of telling the world about my achievements and myself. Till then, Bharat and I would never talk to anyone about our journey together and the things we have achieved. Sachin told us that day that we had to talk about our unique story because it could inspire other people. We were touched when he asked Bharat to be his friend as well. Bharat was taken aback and asked him why he wanted to be friends with a person who had done nothing in life. Sachin told Bharat he had done something unbelievable. He said, 'You don't know the value of time but I do, because I get to spend so little time with my family. You have devoted years of your life to serve someone and that is exemplary. I want to be your friend if you will make me one.'

I have come a long way from the little boy in the hill town of Chikmaglur and today I dream of doing other things with my life. I write poetry in three different languages—English, Hindi, and Urdu—and I am hopeful that someday, they will be published. Because my own journey was so full of struggles, I write about inspiration and about patriotism which is very strong inside me. I want to write books, stories, songs, and through my writings, I want to convey a message that even in the most difficult situations in life, if you hang in there, and wait for the right moment, there is hope and an opportunity waiting around the corner so that you can show your worth to the world.

Having gone through years of struggle, I am now at a stage where I want to live each moment to the fullest. I love movies, sports, classical music concerts, and cricket, and even though it annoys and saddens me that the disabled in India continue to have no access to all these places, I am hopeful that things will change some day.

My friendship with Bharat has only strengthened in the last few years. When I joined Mphasis, Bharat said he was dropping his plans to continue his studies because he thought that at 22, he had missed the boat. I would not stand that thought and at my insistence, he signed up for his engineering course and is now an engineer working with HP. He is my companion, the friend who believes that there is nothing I cannot do, the man who will argue with security guards and authorities who managed sports stadiums or malls because none of them are accessible to me by wheelchair. He says that he is not just fighting for me but for all the people like me. 'Change might not come immediately but if we keep talking about these issues, the change will eventually happen,' he says.

I am blessed our story has a happy ending.

George Abraham

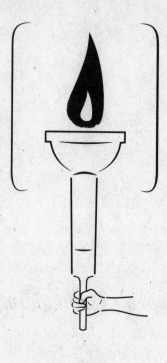

George Abraham is perhaps best represented by the symbol of a torchbearer (also relates to the honour bestowed upon him in the Atlanta Olympics). Holding the torch high signifies the dignity he commands for himself and for his community, also marking him as a champion for the wide and varied service he has selflessly imparted over the years. The flame could mean the flame of passion and flame of consciousness for most people in the society who do not have the right perspective to look at disability.

The handle of the torch bears the shape of a cricket bat, bringing about his brilliant idea of developing the personality of blind through the means of cricket.

In the early 60s, in the sleepy town of Hubli, an adolescent boy who stood along with his classmates at the starting block for a 100-meter run was asked by his teacher why he even bothered to participate in the race since he was always among the last to touch the finish line when the event wrapped up. The boy was unwavering in his determination to participate, insisting that he loved to run and did not care if he came last in the race. But that day , at the semi-finals, he ran as if his life depended on it, reaching the finishing line ahead of the entire group of runners. Jubilant, he headed towards the starting bock for the finals, only to run into the same teacher who promptly asked him what he was doing on the track all over again. This time, the boy pulled himself up proudly and asked the teacher to look at the list of winners of the previous race. His name would be at the top of the list, he told her with quiet pride.

And from then onwards, for the next three years, the boy was the fastest in school, leaving other contestants behind by yards as they raced to the finishing line. At 4.30 am every day, he would be at the engineering college ground near his house, running up the hills surrounding the town, pushing himself till he was happy he had made the cut.

It never mattered to the boy, George Abraham, that being visually impaired was a burden or a hurdle in life. In the decades since then, George has charted a journey for himself that has proved to him at every step that being blind is not a limiting factor. In fact, his entire life is proof that everything is possible if we put our minds to it. After years of a very successful career in advertising, he walked away from it to bring about a change in the way the world sees and treats visually impaired people. 'Being blind is not a problem, people's mind-set about the blind is the tragedy,' he says.

'I realized, early on, that it was all about orientation and practice. It is about making an adjustment, bringing your own strategies into play. You'll have a different way of doing it, but you will still do it. And that's my philosophy in life, too. Everything can be done, but no two people can be expected to perform the same way. Let them do it their way.'

At an event in Mumbai a couple of years ago, I was the last speaker at the end of a rather long day of intense speeches. It was raining outside so when I walked on to the stage, I began my presentation with the song, 'Listen to the falling rain' by Jose Feliciano. When I sang the first verse, there was stunned silence, and I told the audience, 'I've sung this song for three reasons: 1) It's raining outside and Mumbai is always special when it is raining. 2) This song is sung by Jose Feliciano who also happens to be blind. 3) I also sang this song because when we speak of professional engagements for blind people, we always consider music as one of the possibilities. The moment somebody's blind, we immediately think of teaching him music. I told the audience that music and blindness actually have no connection at all—it's all a myth.'

When I finished telling them my three reasons for singing, I was met with thunderous applause from the audience. For me, the biggest stumbling block for the visually impaired is not the fact that they can't see but the fact that people think that they are not capable of anything much because they can't see.

My own journey of working to make this a better world for the blind and the visually impaired started some time in 1988-89 when I visited a school for the blind for the first time in my life. I was shocked and disheartened at the sight of so many blind and partially blind young people languishing there. The conditions in which they were living and studying were so pathetic that I asked the management of the place what future these blind people could look forward to. The indifferent response I got was even more shocking: 'Poor chaps, they're blind. Some of them might go to university, but many of them will just end up at by the wayside with little to do. What can they possibly do? They are blind.'

It was then that I realized how lucky I was to have had the best possible education and parents who actually saw my potential and invested in my future. We were two brothers and I was never treated differently because of my disability. Our parents addressed my academic, physical, spiritual, and emotional needs very well, never ever expecting a little less from me because I was blind.

The incident at the blind school was possibly the turning point of my life. I was 30 years of age and had spent almost a decade working with an advertising agency but there was a nagging sense of restlessness in me. I wanted to do more with my life. I decided that I should use my time and my energies to focus on figuring out ways to dispel the myths around blindness and creating more opportunities for them to live as equals in society.

Thankfully for me, my wife was more than happy to partner with me in my vision and we decided that it is better to do things when we still had the energy instead of waiting for retirement to do what we were passionate about. My knowledge of this space at that point was very limited and the only resource I had was my own life but it was not a bad resource at all because I, myself, had grown up in the world of the blind and had made something out of myself despite the impairment.

I had grown up with a set of parents who encouraged me every step of the way. My father's civil engineering job meant that we spent large parts of our lives in various small towns across India, including Hubli, which is where I really found my moorings. My mother's constant positivity had kept me on my toes, taking me through the years after school, when I first left my home to study at the prestigious St. Stephen's College in Delhi. I loved every bit of the college experience, graduating in Mathematics and going on to do a post-graduate degree in Operations Research. I never knew that just around the corner was what was, looking back, some of the worst years of my life. It was after my post graduation that I realized the hard reality of being blind in a country where it is considered a curse and a burden. After knocking on several doors, I soon realized that all my qualifications would not get me a job, simply because I was blind. I was so disheartened that I packed my bags one day and went back to my hometown in Kerala, where my retired father lived. It was a harrowing time. I hated the pity and the cynicism of family and friends who constantly told me that I was expecting too much from life, considering that I was blind. I moped and pitied myself till one morning, I woke up and said to myself that it was time I took charge of my own life and made things happen. I left that day and returned to Delhi and within a few days, I had got my first job at an advertising agency—a profession which I followed for almost a decade until destiny took me to the blind school where I was forced to soul search once more.

When I decided to leave my career and work with the blind, I became my own benchmark because if I could become what I am from where I came from, then I said to myself that could be a possible route for other people, too.

A meeting with an official in the Ministry of Social Justice and Empowerment gave me the direction I needed when he said it was a good idea for me to travel around the country to see what organizations working in this space were doing. The time I spent travelling around the country—Mumbai, Bengaluru, Delhi, and other cities—was an eye-opener. Early one morning at the National Institute for the Visually Handicapped (NIVH) at Dehradun, I woke to the sound of cricket commentary and decided to go have a closer look. What I saw astonished me. It was a group of kids playing cricket with a ball that rattled while the wicket keeper kept up a steady commentary on the game. Obviously the commentary was not very accurate because he could not see what was going on but what was very evident was that everyone was immensely enjoying the game. I was amazed at the skill displayed because the batsmen were actually connecting when they swung at the balls thrown at them, the fielders were adept at stopping the ball, and the bowling was largely accurate. There might have been a certain amount of seeing involved, but primarily, the entire game was based on hearing and it was a perfect example of hand-ear coordination instead of hand-eye coordination. It was inspiring to watch them and when I spoke to their instructors, I was told that the kids played cricket every time they got a chance during the day. I realized then that this game could be a wonderful tool to develop the personality of the blind.

Sports teach us so much, including teamwork, leadership, planning, strategy, group dynamics, ambition, initiative, and physical fitness. It came to me, that with the kind of following cricket has in India, it could actually be a wonderful medium of communicating the ability and talent of the visually impaired to the world. Because what you see on the cricket field is far different from the stereotypical image of a blind person.

As a partially seeing person, I had played cricket up to a certain level during my childhood but had to give it up reluctantly when the bowling became really fast and we moved from using tennis balls to hard balls. I always used to dream of being a fast bowler as a kid but when I realized that my eyesight would never allow me to become that, I gave up that dream. But when I saw those blind kids playing cricket, all my childhood passion and energy came back and I told myself that I would promote this sport as a way of spreading the word about the abilities of the blind. The journey started in 1990 with a National Cricket Tournament where nineteen teams of blind cricketers played against each other for top honours and it eventually led me to establish the World Blind Cricket Council in 1996.

The cricket teams that came and participated in the games were generated by the NGOs who work with the blind because that's where blind people congregate. For the NGOS, my cricket project was not a priority because they had activities of their own to fund and so, they would give me assistance from project to project, subject to availability of funds. For me, this meant that I still had to run around through the year to generate funds for the cricket events. It was tough because I was trying to get sponsors to look at this as an event to be sponsored as opposed to something they were donating to. For me, the logic is simple: sponsorship recognizes ability while donation recognizes disability. People donate to you because you are working with the blind. I was trying to bring about a shift in the mind-set of people and even though I don't know to what extent I might have succeeded, Coca Cola sponsored the event from 1993-1998 which was a big breakthrough for us.

Slowly the idea caught the imagination of the country and I started dreaming of the next big step for me. I was already neck-deep in my work with the visually handicapped till one day, I actually started talking about the possibility of organizing a World Cup cricket tournament for the blind. In 1994, at the age of 33, I got the Sanskriti Award for Young Leadership in the Field of Social Development, in recognition of my work with the visually handicapped. The Sanskriti Sansthan believes that winners of the award have the potential to become leaders of the future so when I got the award, it got me a lot of media attention. That was fortuitous for me because after that, a couple of people joined my organization and got seriously involved in my project.

In November 1998, when seven nations from across four continents fought to take home the first ever World Cup in Cricket for the Blind, it was not just a dream come true for me but an honour for the country as well—no other country had done this before and no one had ever thought it possible to pull off such a feat. For me, it was a reiteration of what I had believed in all along: that nothing is impossible in this world if we decide to keep away our fears and cynicism, and open our hearts to the potential in the lives of people.

My preoccupation with enhancing the quality of life of the blind continued unabated.

The Kanishka World Cup opened a lot of doors for me. After an event where I spoke about inclusive education one day, representatives of the British Airways got in touch with me, telling me they would like to work with me on some project. They wanted me to talk about my experiences with my disability and how I forged ahead in life despite it. I told them that one of the things which I'd like to do is to travel around the country and conduct sensitization and personality development workshops for young blind boys and girls. They agreed instantly and for the next few months, I travelled to Mumbai, Bengaluru, Trivandum, Trichur, Calicut, Aligarh, Goa, Gangavati among other places, conducting almost forty workshops, where I delivered motivational talks about the importance of communication, among other things.

The blind in India have traditionally lived like frogs in wells. Their knowledge and awareness of the world is limited to the school or the institute they live in and typically, the attitude of the people who run these schools is that they are being charitable in imparting education to their students. Of course, they say that education is empowering but the fact of the matter is that the quality of education is not good enough because they are not accountable to anyone. The result is that these blind students grow up in a vacuum with little exposure or interaction with the outside world. To me, education is not just about learning Math, Science, or Physics but also about what you learn by interacting with peers on a daily basis. Education is also about skills of communication, logic, reasoning, analysis, research, and about social etiquettes that we pick up by our interaction with those around us. I found that the blind person was being denied these kinds of opportunities because he lived in his little world which was the blind school. During my travel, I also met people in the media, bureaucracy, education, and everywhere, the perception about blind people was that they were lesser beings and any work which is done with them is a noble activity. 'Oh wonderful, you are working with the blind, great!' In that one sentence, I realized the problem is not with the blindness, it was with the mind-set of people and I felt it was imperative to address that issue. Even today, the real problem we face, the real reason why quality services aren't available, the real reason why parents get rattled when they discover that their child is blind or if somebody loses eyesight, is that they're not aware of the possibilities there are in a life of blindness.

In 2002, I set up SCORE (Society For Communication and Research), a voluntary organization that would commit itself to projects with the blind by giving them the opportunity to develop, to be rehabilitated, and to be socially integrated.

People with visual impairment are usually treated with pity and charity in our country. It is tragic that instead of focussing on their ability and potential, we focus on their limitations, and this leads to their marginalization in society. Instead of looking at them as potential human resource for a developing country, most people end up treating them as liabilities. When I set up the Score Foundation, it was to correct these concepts about the blind and that eventually led to Project Eyeway , a one-stop knowledge resource about living life with vision impairment that disseminates information through a network of resources, including a dedicated helpdesk, a radio show, website, SMS alerts, workshops, and an audio books initiative.

There are over 16 million blind and 28 million visually impaired people in India who are often marginalized and Eyeway works towards getting them equal rights, responsibilities, and opportunities to help them lead fulfilling, independent, economic, and socially productive lives.

Every day, we work to minimize discrimination towards the visually impaired community and towards empowering them with knowledge and information so that they can live a dignified life and become contributing members of society. You will be surprised at how many calls and emails the staff at Eyeway field get everyday from blind people who are in distress and we do our best by counselling and guiding such callers to the best of our abilities.

But what is equally true is that there are thousands of enthusiastic and inspired blind people who want to make more out of their lives. Disability is God-given but a handicap is man-made. It is up to us whether or not we let disability hold us back from realizing our dreams. At Eyeway, part of our work is advocacy and sensitization of various stakeholders—including bodies such as the Planning Commission and the government—so that we can change the way people perceive the blind. The government, the planning commission, the ministries, even parents will start investing in their children when we begin talking about people with disability as a potential resource. The crux of the matter is that when you invest in people, you expect returns but when you donate or provide, as you do for the blind, you don't expect any return. The majority of people do not see the value of expectations and the attitude of people generally is: 'After all, he's blind, what can he do?' That has to change.

One of the projects that we did to dispel the myth that the blind can't do anything is Nazar Ya Nazariya, a 13-part serial that runs on Doordarshan to showcase some inspiring real-life stories of the blind or visually impaired. After each of these telecasts, we are inundated with calls and emails from viewers who tell us how surprised and admiring they are that a blind person is able to do such extraordinary things with his life.

Now that the Score Foundation and Eyeway are established and running seamlessly, I have the urge to do something more with my own life. Setting up these organizations and getting attached to them has kept me bound to it for long with concerns about funding and paying salaries etc. But I realize now that in getting bound to it, I am actually not doing half the things that I want to do in other fields.

At 55 years, my time on this earth is limited and my ideas are personal and very unique to me. I'm now ready to take on the next chapter of my life so that I can be a living example of what a blind person can achieve. My primary passions in life over the years have been communication in the spoken and written forms but new, innovative forms are available today for me to pursue. Who knows, I might get into filmmaking, do a travel show for the blind, or take up consulting assignments that allow me to execute my ideas through them, rather than trying to do it all by myself.

As a child, I had three dreams—I wanted to be a fast bowler like Dennis Lillie, have a presence like Amitabh Bachchan, and sing like Kishore Kumar. I achieved the first dream through my cricket project. I can never be Amitabh but I think, in my own way, I have created a body of work which has given me a definitive niche in society. I am now on the way to fulfil my third dream by learning singing from the Delhi School of Music. My belief is, if you have a skill, use it. You don't have to toe the conventional line. At a Christian organization in Germany where I was asked to speak about devotion, I ended my speech by singing a song. A couple of days later, I was surprised when there was a public request for me to sing one more time, at the same venue! Who knows, I might just end up making a music video…that's the kind of person I am. If I have an idea, I have to pursue it till I make it happen. I dreamt of spreading the word about the abilities and latent talent of the blind and made this happen by producing the radio programme, 'Eyeway: yeh hai roshni ka karawan,' that aired on Vividh Bharti across India and FM Rainbow Delhi.

There are other things that I want to do as well. The rapid changes that have happened in technology, the advent of global media, and other factors that have resulted in a gradual erosion of values as we have known it in our times. We are living in a world where if you like something, you just grab it. And if you don't get it, you react by throwing acid on it, something that did not happen fifty years ago. The spiritual side of my life has played a very important role in making the man I am today. A lot of things I do is because of my faith in God and I want to play a role in bringing that faith back into the lives of the younger generation. Given the conditions in which we live and work, I think the next generation will have a lot of intellectual and emotional problems. Anxiety and disturbed minds will be a thing of the future and when that happens, spiritual strength is what will help them cope with such problems.

My own story has been one of following my heart and treading the path of what I thought was the right way. When I left my job to work with the blind, it was a bold and reckless thing to do, especially because we were expecting our first baby. But my wife, Rupa, and I were young and able to rough it out, travelling all over the country and putting our minds together to do something that would change the way we deal with the visually impaired. My wife took up a job as a horticulturist so that I could focus on this goal fully.

Both of us were very happy despite the fact that the comforts of our lives had disappeared. What was more important was that we were actually doing things that we wanted to do. It was around that time that I saw the blind boys playing cricket in Dehradun, and I started the cricket project.

From that point onwards, life has evolved with a series of new ideas that took me into newer, uncharted areas. I never imagined that what started as a dream shared by two idealistic young people would grow so much and that my team and I would eventually organize two world cup cricket events. We also led our cricket teams to Pakistan and England and the world sat up and took notice. Then, I stepped down from the post of President of the World Blind Cricket Council, an elected body, in 2004 and withdrew from my engagement with cricket in India, handing over the baton to my friend in Bengaluru, G K Mahantesh. The decision was made because it was tough doing so many things at the same time. Also, I realized that unlike commercial cricket, blind cricket doesn't get support very easily and generating funds was a big challenge. The cricket project is now held by the Bengaluru-based NGO Samarthanam trust which held the T20 championships for blind cricket a couple of years ago.

What I've learnt is that if you hold things close to your heart, they don't grow. You have got to let go at the right time so that other people take it and run. And you have the personal satisfaction of seeing the thing that you started grow—it's almost like watching your baby.

Looking back, there have been many milestones in my life and each of them has taught me something. In 1969, when I won my first elocution competition in 4th grade, speaking about Bal Gangadhar Tilak at my school in Hubli, it was the most exciting thing to happen.

Then, when I was in 9th grade, I managed to beat the fastest runners in my school despite the fact that I was a fat, blind kid, who would always be last at the finishing line.

For me, the entire journey has been interesting. I was very ambitious, but for some strange reason, I was not really interested in big money. I was more interested in making a mark, in making a contribution. When I got the Sanskriti Award, I was very excited because people were writing about me but being famous was not my goal. As a child, I wanted to do things which I loved doing, doing them well, and I wanted to be famous. I don't want to be famous anymore but I still like to do things that I love doing.

At each stage, life brings you to various points that work to motivate you. For me, one of these moments came when I was given the extraordinary honour of running with our

Olympic torch at the Atlanta Olympics in the year 1996. A representative of Coca-Cola called late one night enquiring if I had a US visa. I did not have one at the time but I asked him why he wanted to know. I was stumped when he said that the company was sponsoring a group of five people from India to go to the US and run with the torch. I told the man I would try and get a visa but I had just under 24 hours before my flight to the US was to take off. I called up the embassy that very moment and explained the situation to them. They said if I could get a bank draft of Rs 700 and my application to them before 9 am, they could help. Since banks did not open before 9 am, there was no way I could get a draft and so, I simply gathered a bunch of the articles that appeared about me in the media and landed up at the embassy with the cash and my application. The visa officer was intrigued when I told him about my work with cricket for the blind and by the media coverage that spoke about my work. I had my visa within five minutes of submitting my application and I was at the airport well in time to board my 5 pm flight! The story does not end there. I had called up a friend at Liberty Shoes, telling him I was to run with the Olympic torch and asking if his company wanted to sponsor my shoes since I did not own a pair of running shoes. To my surprise, when I got to the airport, there was a guy there from Liberty Shoes with five pairs of shoes to choose from. When I ran with the torch at Atlanta, pretty much the only thing that I had of my own was my underwear! The shorts and the t-shirt were given by the International Olympic Association. Running with the Olympic torch was one of the most inspiring and memorable events in my life.

There were other memorable events after that such as the day I managed to get the first World Cup Cricket for the Blind off the ground in 1998 and when I was chosen by the Limca Book of Records as one of the five people of the year in 2007, along with luminaries such as A.R. Rehman, Mahesh Bhupathi, Dr Devi Shetty, and Mary Kom, the boxer. Equally, another high point was the way we envisioned and put together our television serial, *Nazar ya Nazariya*.

One of the things that I have learnt over the span of my life is that if you believe in something, you have got to make it happen. Don't wait for things to happen to you. Instead, make your moves and make them happen. And, always keep your objectives in mind because it is easy to get distracted and go off the course.

My years spent working with the blind, often asking for funds to continue my work, taught me that humility is the most important value to cultivate. Pride and ego are things that will destroy you. Sometimes, hardships makes us forget our values but I believe in always being true to my values and being honest and sincere because you can defend honesty, but not dishonesty. When you achieve something by honest means, that feeling of achievement is far greater.

My mother passed away at the age of 42, succumbing to cancer, when I was a mere 21 years old and a few months short of finishing my masters' degree. She had always wanted to write the story of my life and to this day, it hurts that she passed away before she could see what her son achieved in life. My dad was excited when I started working on the World Cup Cricket for the Blind, but even he passed away before the event could be held in 1998. Sometimes, things don't pan out the way we want them to.

Today, I have learnt that when something closes on you, that could very well be the beginning of something new, which is more exciting. It is like you take a diversion from a roadblock and you suddenly discover something very exciting on the way, so you stop there and do something new.

So if there's a challenge, resolve it. Challenges are there to teach you, to show you the way, rather than to block you. Today, I am clear that that I don't want to work with blind people; I want to work with non-blind people because it is they who need to change their mind-sets so that the blind are mainstreamed. Score Foundation and Eyeway are the results of that belief. In the future, if I start making films and travelling around, and engaging in the rest of the world, I hope every person I engage with will be impacted by my own life story . My core agenda is the same, of changing perceptions. Away from my work, I enjoy spending time with my family, going out for movies, films, and holidays, along with my two daughters, Neha and Tara.

Looking back, my life has been an incredibly exciting journey but I am nowhere close to being content. I believe there are exciting things yet to happen in the times to come…

Girisha H.N.

The sketch tries to express the aspiration of Girisha. As he says, 'It is not just about hitting the golden number of 1.68 metres jump but to touch the sky.' Hence, a successful jump over the pole which is really his performance of the past and then we have a great take-off that puts him at the loftiest heights—in the sky—above the clouds and birds (a reflection of his determination and a position that he may soon acquire in the next Olympics).

But for the sheer brilliance of his talent and his complete confidence in himself, Girisha H.N. could have remained one of the thousands of young people who grow up in villages all over India, who don't get the chances that their more privileged counterparts in big cities get.

Girisha was born with a disfigured leg but not once did he allow that to be the most important part of his life. Growing up in a tiny village where even a pair of slippers were a luxury for most people, he developed a ruggedness that allowed him to run around barefoot and win every competition in school, despite his physical constraint. He climbed trees, grazed cattle on the hills surrounding the village, and raced fearlessly downhill on a battered cycle which he loved. Even as a child, he had a hunger to better himself and win every race or competition that he ran with his friends. It was perhaps, this determination to rise above his circumstances that eventually led him to the winners' podium to receive the silver medal in men's high jump at the Paralympic Games in London, in 2012. The diminutive young man with a shy smile and a burning desire to bring glory to his country finally achieved his dream on faraway shores and when he did that, it re-instilled hope in the hearts of others like him, who struggle against all odds to get to where he did.

I met Girisha one evening at the Kanteerava stadium

in Bengaluru where he began his journey towards getting international sporting success a few years ago. This was also where he walked away from the sport after crushing disappointments led him to believe that sports could never be a meaningful occupation for anyone in this country. He had to look after his ageing parents and he could not do that without a job. It was only the dogged determination of his coach and his own self-belief that brought him back to the stadium in time to make the cut for the Paralympics, where he created history in 2012.

'At just 1.68 metres, I am told I am short for a high jumper but that means nothing to me because my ambition touches the sky,' Girisha said to me that evening. 'My next goal, my current dream, is crystal clear to me. At the next Paralympics in Rio, 2016, I want the gold medal.'

I was born on 26th January, India's Republic Day, in Hosanagara village in Karnataka's Hassan district, and if someone were to have told me during my childhood years that I would one day be awarded a Padmashri by the President of my country, I would never have believed it. Nor would anyone in the village because there was little chance that anybody could make anything out of their lives there, other than eke out a living. The bolder, luckier ones escaped to the big cities where they had a better chance of making a life for themselves.

I was not conscious of the significance of my date of birth when I was a child, but all through my adolescent years, I have had this feeling that my destiny is connected inexorably to the destiny of my country.

Not that anything in my childhood suggested that I could achieve any greatness. We come from very humble stock. My father is from an even tinier village in Karnataka where his family worked on their small piece of land to run the household. Later, when a dam was planned in the locality, the government acquired my father's land and gave him another piece of land as compensation. I was born there in a humble house with bright red Mangalore tiles, in a hilly area set on the backwaters of the Cauvery river.

I studied in a school at Hosanagara till 4th grade and because the village did not have a school for further studies, we walked to a larger village, Marianagara, 2 kms away so I could take the bus to my new school which was 10 kms away. The Christian school we went to was very strict and after school hours, the bench leader would go over our work with us. We would leave home at 8 am and the plan was to take the last bus at 6.30 pm to go back home. But revision of our lessons by the bench leaders often meant that I missed the bus and would have to hitch a ride on a tempo or walk all the way home. My elder sister was my companion on this journey.

In the village, no one had the luxury of footwear to walk around. After 6th grade, I got a pair of leather sandals made by the local cobbler and when I got my first pair of Hawaii slippers to wear to college, I felt like a prince. Childhood was a time of happy memories when we hung about with the local boys, swimming in the canals, and fishing. Even at that point, I was fascinated by high jump. My friends would hold ropes on both sides and I would jump over the rope, higher and higher, as my friends looked on in astonishment. Since we had very limited means, our house did not have power supply and we studied under the light of kerosene lamps. I would inevitably come home only after the lamps were lit because I would go straight from school to join gangs of village boys and race against each other, running to beat the wind. Even though I had strength in only one leg, I beat them and that gave me the confidence that I could do what everyone else could do. I never thought I had any disability. I wanted to better the performance of anyone who competed with me and I wanted to win.

Often, I would take the cattle out to graze in the mountains or in the forests because that gave me full scope to roam around unfettered, to swim in the backwaters, climb trees, run around without being supervised by the adults. The region grew potatoes, ginger, paddy, and maize and I learnt the ropes of working in the fields from my father. Even today, I continue to be a farmer at heart.

When my parents were not looking, I would un-spool my father's collection of music tapes so that my friends would hold it on both sides and I would jump, higher and higher. My great-grandfather would chase me with a stick, all around the house, because I had destroyed his favourite music tapes. I would only jump after all my friends had finished their turn and my first jump was, even at the age of 8, higher than their best effort. I was only a little boy in class 2nd grade then.

As a kid, I was very naughty and spent all day—before and after school—swimming in the river, playing *lagori* (seven stones), *marbles*, and *malkoti* and clambering up tall coconut trees. Every day, I got a thrashing from my father and I think my first lessons in high jump came from jumping over the fence surrounding my house, when my father chased me with a stick. My father would keep me from going out with friends, or swimming alone in the canal, because he worried that I would get up to all kinds of pranks and hurt myself. My elder sister, only two years older than me, was like my mother, breaking up fights and taking up for me even with the village bullies.

As a kid, I was fascinated with bicycles but my father did not like me to use the old bicycle parked in our courtyard. He worried I would fall off and hurt myself. I would take the old bicycle every day and ride fast on a down slope but since I had never learnt to brake, I would simply jump off the bicycle when I wanted to stop. It was not the safest thing to do and often my sister would complain to my parents about my doings. The inevitable thrashing landed on me but I did not mind it as long as I could have my way! Often, I would threaten my sister that I would thrash her if she carried tales to my father but she did it anyway.

That is how it is in the villages even today. Since there was no television, radio, or video games to distract or entertain us, we kept ourselves busy with other activities. And without electricity at home, we went to bed early, by 9 pm, which meant that we woke up early and so I could get up to mischief in the mornings, too, before setting off to school. Some 20-30 of us friends would raid jackfruits from the neighbours' farms and bury them in the ground for ripening. I loved jackfruit and could polish off an entire fruit on my own.

Doing my lessons was not hard for me at all. While my friends laboured over it, I simply sat in the courtyard and read each lesson two times, memorizing it without a single mistake.

My parents say I was born with my foot bent the way it is today. They tried many times to straighten it. Technology was not as advanced as it is today, so the surgeons could never fix my leg but thankfully, they managed to give it a shape which allowed me to walk. But God made sure that it was good for running. He also gave me a fighting spirit.

It was in 7th grade that my school teacher, Lourde Mary, noticed I could jump well. She would watch my sport activities with great interest. I did not know the difference between high jump and long jump. All I knew was that I liked to be on the sports field. She pushed for me to go for a local competitive sport event at Hobli, a small taluka place near our home, because she was convinced that I could compete well even though I was differently-abled. That was the first time I started taking things seriously. My rival was a guy who had three gold medals to his name but it was me who walked away with the silver medal and got selected for the next level of the competition. I thought I had got the moon in my palms when somebody in the audience announced a Rs 20 cash prize specially for me because of my spirit despite being physically challenged. (No, physically challenged is fine. This comment is from him and each person talks about disability in their own words and terminology). It was a big amount for a 12-year-old to win. In the village, small things are special. I've tried singing, dancing, and other activities so that I could get a small prize—even a plastic ball was a huge gift to get. I took part in debating, too, and won the first prize and soon, I was so confident that I lost all my fears and inhibitions.

At the President's award function for Padma Shri awardees in 2013, Prime Minister Manmohan Singh congratulated me for bringing home a silver medal in high jump at the London Paralympics in 2012. Other luminaries from the country, including Mrs Sonia Gandhi, were at the event. I waited my turn patiently to talk to Mr Singh and when he was ready to listen to me, I expressed my anguish about how the government had failed to deliver on its promise of giving me a job—an officer's post at the Sports Authority of India—as was announced immediately after I got the silver medal. I told him it was unfair that all the medal winners at the London Olympics 2012 had already been given prestigious government jobs but when it came to giving the same treatment to medal winners in the Paralympics, the government was dithering. I told him the cash prize which I got from the government was good but that would not last me forever. Giving me a job instead, would ensure that I got to live a life of dignity and respect, and would give me the chance to continue to practice my game. Sadly, two years after I won the medal, I am still waiting for the government to deliver on the promised job. Even the state government has failed to give me a job, despite repeated pleas on my part.

In our state, there is no tradition of encouraging sports (sports in general) but thankfully, things are changing. The Rajiv Gandhi Khel Ratna Award was never given to Paralympians even though Olympic medalists are directly eligible for the prestigious award. Now, thankfully, both Olympians and paralympians will be eligible for the Arjuna and Khel Ratna awards.

When I passed my 7th grade public exam with a first division, it was a big achievement. I was excited to go to high school but soon, that enthusiasm waned because I realized I was not about to get a chance to involve myself in my passion- sports. The school did not believe the disabled can achieve much in sport or in life and they were scared they would be blamed if they allowed me to participate in any sports and I ended up injuring myself. I was very disheartened. I had to watch the action from the sidelines of the sports ground when the rest of my class had a great time on the field. I pleaded with my teachers to allow me to play, too, but to no avail. When nothing worked, I accompanied my classmates to sports competitions, carrying their gear for them—that was how badly I wanted to be on the sports ground. Sometimes I would sneak in to the ground and practice high jumps on my own.

Around this time, I started falling behind in class in math and my father soon sent me to a tuition teacher. I had no idea that this one simple thing would earn me the wrath of my math teacher in school. He saw my taking tuitions as a comment on his (in)ability to teach and every day, I got punished and humiliated in class for this imagined slight. I took to bunking class and would go swimming instead. Just before my 10th grade exams, I injured my leg when a sharp stone pierced my foot as I was running around with my friends, barefoot. The injury soon got septic and doctors at the hospital told my father I would have had to get my foot amputated if he had been a few days late in taking me there. A surgery was undertaken to extract the stone and my condition was so bad that that I had to rest at home for months to recuperate. I was, of course, very happy because this would enable me to appear for my exams from home instead of going to school. Unfortunately for me, I flunked my math paper and had to re-appear after a few months of math tuition all over again. My father was so ashamed of my failing that he went around telling his friends that I had got good marks in other subjects but failed only because of math! His dream was that I would become a teacher one day and flunking my exams was not going to get me to be a teacher!

In some ways, the beginning of my journey into serious sports happened when I passed 10th grade and joined a junior college near Coorg. Here, I finally found people who believed in me and my talent. I shall always be grateful to KB Kempe

Gowda, the principal who was a great support. At a college event, I competed with a state level gold medalist and won against him. Mr Kempe Gowda was so impressed he insisted that I should be encouraged in sports activities because I was able to take on an established sportsperson despite my being a differently-abled person.

During this period, I would practice my jumps in a sand pit in college, all by myself. I had no competition, there was no one to help me, but unknown to me, my principal watched me slog away. My determination impressed him and slowly, he started making sure I got into *taluka* and district level competitions till one day I won a bronze medal at the state level inter-college athletic competition in Dharwad. My joy knew no bounds. My parents were my biggest supporters during the entire period. In 2003-04, I passed my junior college with a first class without even having attended my preparatory exams. My principal was so thrilled he gave me a grand cash prize of Rs 200. In the following months, my confidence peaked when they treated me like a hero and that increased my hunger for more achievements, so that I could earn the trust they placed in me.

When it came to deciding on a college for my bachelor's degree, I joined the AN Vardarajulu college 40 kms away only because it was known for encouraging sports. My initial days there, to my misfortune, proved to be struggle because the Director of Physical Education said it was difficult for the college to change existing rules in order to allow me to compete in the University Athletics Meet. I showed him my jump and all my past achievements and eventually they sent my entry for the Mysore University Athletics Meet at Hassan in 2006. I and a lot of other sportsmen from my college went for the meet well in advance so that we could practice hard. Four days before the event, however, the University's Sports Director informed me that there was no way they could allow a physically-challenged person to participate in the event. My hopes of getting ahead in the sport were dashed to the ground and I was heartbroken. No amount of pleading and begging worked, and I returned from the stadium in tears to board a bus to go back home. Thankfully for me, there were lots of people who believed in my talent and ability.

Upon seeing my despair, my friends took up my case with the Sports Director till he bowed to public pressure and relented. I was overjoyed when my friends arrived at the bus stop where I was awaiting the departure of the bus to take me back home. That day, on that sports ground, I put my entire being into making sure that I would prove my talent to the world. My effort paid back in the form of a bronze medal against an able-bodied sportsman who had won several medals in the past. When I walked away with the medal, the entire stadium was on their feet applauding me and the man who had doubted my ability himself came up and congratulated me. My next goal was winning a national award. Simultaneously, the Paralympic Committee of India wrote to my college asking them to send me for a national competition being held in Bengaluru. It was my first time in a big city and I was frightened. I had lived in a small village all my life and had no clue how to get to the stadium by myself. I used up part of a Rs 2000 scholarship money I had got in college to reach Bengaluru but realized upon my arrival that the event had been postponed by a week and they had forgotten to inform me. With no option but to stay back in the city, I scrimped and scrounged so that I would not run out of my dwindling stock of money. When the day arrived for the competition, I chose to participate in the 100 metres track event and high jump competitions.

I was overconfident and thought I would win the events easily but realized quickly that competing against professional runners was a different ball game altogether—they finished their 100 metres that day before I could even get up to the 50 metre mark on the track. Disheartened, I put my heart into practicing my jumps for three days at a stretch and when the competition day arrived, I cleared every jump at the high jump competition, beating the previous Paralympic national gold medal winner. Such is the irony of life. Just two days before that, I was hungering for a medal that I could take back to the college. I was their hero and was hoping for at least a bronze that I could take back with me to show them but I walked away with a gold, creating a national award in Paralympics in the process. I had managed a 1.68 metres high jump and I was raring to go for more events to demonstrate my skills.

It has been a long and often very disheartening, uphill task to get to where I have been. I have realized that the world only sees your successes, the medals, the articles about you in the media, but they don't see the long hours of practice and the heartbreak when things go up in smoke because of factors beyond your control. I shudder to think what my fate would have been without a job had Herbalife not stepped in and appointed me a brand ambassador after I won the silver medal at the Paralympics. That fee and their sponsorship is enough to make sure that I am able to put my entire energy into practicing for the Rio Paralympics Olympics without having to worry about looking for a job.

In 2008, I was full of spirit and raring to go into the Paralympics, and it was a crippling disappointment for me when the government cleared two other candidates in my category, only because they thought these candidates were more likely to win than I was. And this, despite the fact that I had delivered a career best high jump of 1.80 metres, which cleared me for the qualifying trials for the Beijing Paralympics. I felt lost and betrayed because there was no one who stood by me to fight my case. Eventually, disheartened by the system, I left my sport without a backward glance and tried to pick up the threads of my life by getting myself a job.

In retrospect, I must admit that it was possibly for the best that I did not make it to the 2008 Paralympics. I simply did not have the international exposure or experience to have taken on some of the best sportspersons in the world and there was no way I could have got a medal home. When the Paralympic Committee of India got a chance to hold the AIWA world games in Bengaluru in 2009, I cleared my jump with a 1.72 metres in the F44 category and got the bronze medal. Both the sports authorities and I were woefully ignorant of the categorization of sportspersons with varying degrees of disability. We did not know that those in the F42 categories have a higher degree of disability and a point system gives them some advantage to win a game. I realized that I should have been put in the F42 category and was disappointed after that incident by the lack of support from the government and their indifference to crucial matters concerning sports. Sport is not an easy thing to pursue for anybody, especially from those from humble, rural backgrounds. I could not afford the training gear and other investments required to pursue my passion. I was the eldest in the family and I knew they hoped that their son would be able to support them in their old age. It finally dawned on me that the harsh realities of a career in sports would never allow me to do my duty towards me family. This made me walk away from my dream, even though I breathed and lived sports inside me.

In the years in-between, I completed my Bachelor of Arts and in 2010, I was back in Bengaluru learning English, computer skills, and Business Process Outsourcing training. There were endless rounds of knocking on doors for employment, many job interviews, and countless disappointments. There were opportunities in the BPO sector but my heart was not in doing a job in a BPO because I felt I was qualified to do much more with my life. After an endless struggle, I got my break with ING Vysya Bank in 2011, and I soon got a job in their back office support department. I took the job because I had the consolation of being able to tell people that I worked in a bank and that made me feel good. Thankfully for me, that is also where I met my boss, Mr Rajan, a wonderful man who kept me going when I threatened to quit because I felt my work was no longer fulfilling and deserving of my qualification. 'Good things happen to people who hang on', he would say and I would listen to him because he was like a trusted brother.

In early January 2012, a day that will forever stay etched on my mind, my coach Satyanarayana and some of my friends called, telling me I should get back to sport and try to qualify for the Paralympics in 2012. I approached my boss and impressed upon him how important it was for me to take this last chance to get glory for my country. Rajan sir knew how much sports meant to me and within a short span of time he had garnered around Rs 1 lakh from the ING Vysya Foundation to help me buy my kit and support me in my attempt to qualify for the Paralympics. He said that if I got a gold medal for India, the bank would immediately give me a permanent job. I was thrilled to hear this. A permanent job at the bank would mean a three-fold increase in my salary so I trained feverishly for the event. At the Kuwait Paralympics event which would automatically qualify me for the London Paralympics later that year, I got myself a gold medal. It was unbelievable because I had not practiced for over a year and never expected to get such a breakthrough.

Back at the bank, my employers were happy to have a gold medalist in their fold but my heart was elsewhere—I wanted to be in the Indian contingent that went to the London Olympics. A few days later, I heard news that disturbed me—the government had sent out a notice that all the twenty-five athletes who were selected for the London Paralympics Olympic games would have to report for the training camp in the run up to the London event. This was because the International Paralympic Committee (IPC) had only allotted a quota of five physically challenged sportspersons from India for the event and the government would only send those athletes who had participated in the camp. My heart sank when I realized I would have to choose between my job and my dream of competing at the London Paralympics.

My friends and family dissuaded me from giving up my job for a possible entry into the Paralympics. They pointed out that sports had never given me anything in life but disappointment while my job could change the future of our entire family. But my coach Satyanarayana pointed out that this had always been the dream of my adult life. Another job would always come along but the Paralympics would only come around once in four years. He told me it was a privilege to be selected to represent the country.

Without any thought for the future, I went up to my bosses and tendered my resignation. They were taken aback and dissuaded me saying that they would give me time off from work every day for training and that it was not necessary for me to go to the training camp since I was already qualified for the Paralympics. Sadly, they never understood that it was a now-or-never situation for me. I felt torn because it was hard for me to forget that they had stood by me in my darkest hour by giving me a job and later helping me make my bid for the Kuwait games. I tried telling them that I would get back to work after the Paralympics were over. I finally left the job after serving a month's notice. The day I left, my boss came over and told me he would follow my future life closely because I was like a brother to him. When I was leaving, I was humiliated by taunts from a few colleagues who said I would end up with nothing in my life because sports never gives anything to anyone in this country. Infuriated, I told them that I would prove them wrong and that one day, they would see my name splashed all over because I had brought glory to my country.

For the next few days, my life was all about making sure I got into the list of the five people who would be sent to the Paralympics out of the twenty-five who qualified for the prestigious event. I practically lived on the training ground where I was helped by Satyanarayana, my Romanian coach,

Evgeny Nikitin, and my other mentor, Sahaana. In July 2012, when I cleared a jump of 1.70 metres at the final selection trials in Bengaluru, I jumped to number four in the world ranking and to my utter joy, I found my name in the list of the five athletes who would represent the country. I had never thought I would get that far but having got into that list, I was determined that I would make sure I would get a medal back home.

Over my years in athletics, I had noticed that my peers and colleagues never talked about winning a medal at the Paralympics. It was almost as if it was just enough for them to be able to participate in it! I wanted to change that mind-set.

I remember the days at the Basildon Sports Village in the UK, just before the Olympic games were to take off. I kept my mind focused on the thought that I would win a medal. This was the biggest opportunity in my life and I made sure my mind was focused on good music, positive thoughts, and meditation. I would be pitted against the best athletes in the world and if I made it here, there would be no looking back for me. In practice sessions, I cleared a jump of 1.75 metres for a record five successive times but my real test would come only on the big day.

India got off to a very discouraging start when the Paralympics kicked off in end-August. Things looked completely bleak as athlete after athlete returned to their rooms empty-handed. September 3rd was our last chance to get a medal. When the Indian team captain Jagsher Singh, who was the Asian Long Jumping champ, too, came back to the room without a medal, the entire contingent pinned their hopes on me. And when I leapt the 1.74 metres to get the silver medal, it was not just my dream come true but that of an entire nation. In the few minutes before we started the event, I kept telling myself that it was now up to me to make sure the Indian team left with our heads held high. When my name went up on the board as one of the winners, a crowd of 80,000 people were applauding but my heart leapt in joy when I saw hundreds of Indian flags waving happily in the crowd. My coach, Satyanarayana, had tears in his eyes when the Prince of Denmark awarded me the medal. For one night, Girisha was a hero to the nation and my joy grew manifold when the original heroes, Sachin Tendulkar and Saina Nehwal, said in media interviews that I was an inspiration to the entire country. That alone made all my struggles seem worth it.

From being a naughty little boy in a village to a silver medallist at the Paralympics, it has been a momentous journey. Every time I have reached a goal, I have always thought ahead about my next award. At each step I have motivated myself. My next goal, my current dream, is crystal clear to me. At the Paralympics in Rio, I want the gold medal.

I never thought of myself as disabled. I am differently-abled. From the beginning of my life, I have had big dreams and have focused on making them come true. Medals and awards are not important. What is important is to participate and compete. If you don't win today, you can always get a medal tomorrow. Putting in my best at everything is the most important thing for me. Before I won the silver medal at the Paralympics, nobody knew me or cared about the event. My win has ensured that Paralympics is now known and acknowledged.

The national flag will fly high at the Rio Olympics and I hope to have the gold medal on my neck when the beloved national anthem plays.

Hans Dalal

The art gives form to one of the most important themes of the story - rising above the disability to take up the profession of a tiger conservationist which most people in their best of abilities would dread to imagine. His hands with broken lines come together with a gentle protective care (almost like preserving the flame of a lamp)...and in the centre is the tiger, subtly brought about by its footprint rather than blatantly showing its face. The wave is possibly the sound waves which relates to his long time profession...and creates a sense of visual tension and contrast with the black and white shades (giving vitality to the art).

Hans Dalal's earliest memory is of being hung upside down by the doctors who were treating him at an orthopaedic hospital in Mumbai. Afflicted by cerebral palsy—(Cerebral palsy is defined as set of permanent disorders of the development of movement and posture, leading to limitation in mobility, that are attributed to non-progressive disturbances that occurred in the developing fetal or infant brain. This is also often accompanied by difficulties with thinking, learning, feeling, communication.) within just days of his birth, the little boy had not yet started walking at 5 years of age and had only just about starting to talk. His parents were frantic because all the painstaking trips to therapists did not make their son walk. One fine day, when his mother took him to the hospital, the doctor sent her out of the room and proceeded to hang him upside down. When he protested, the doctor asked him, 'Will you walk if we put you down?' The little boy knew when he was outwitted and said to them that he would, if they first got his mother into the room. 'So then they called my mom and I went tottering to her and thus began my journey. That's one of my earliest memories—it's a weird memory, but it is vivid in my mind,' he says today.

That was perhaps the turning point of his young life. From then on, he lived like other children his age, running around and playing in the compound of his apartment block, falling down often because of his condition but always up on his feet and back to the game. Studies did not interest him and he was terrible at math, but music fascinated him. From infancy, he grew up listening to his father's eclectic collection of music—native African, native North American, jazz, Indian classical, western classical, oldies, rock… His mother encouraged him to learn the keyboard because that was good for his fingers which were affected by the cerebral palsy. He could never become the musician he wanted to be because of his poor motor control but he never imagined that a passion for sound engineering would take him to the other side of the world, to study the science at the Royal Melbourne Institute of Technology, in Australia.

But what uplifts this extraordinary young man's soul today is another kind of music altogether. Instead of the beats of techno, rock, or indie music, his senses soar to the sound of silence in the mountains, the low growl of a tiger, the flapping of wings of a dozen birds as they take flight, and the gentle whisper of a forest breeze.

I saw my first tiger in the wild at the Kanha National Park in 2007, and it was love at first sight. I knew at that moment that I had changed forever in some ways and that I wanted to spend my life in proximity to these magnificent animals for the rest of my life. It would be a different life from the urban jungle in which I lived, but I was determined to do it, no matter what.

Sometimes I think that each of us comes into this world for a specific purpose. What else can explain why I pushed myself to extreme limits to overcome my disability from cerebral palsy to study sound engineering but spend my entire time now in pursuit of these beautiful cats?

When I came back from that visit to Kanha, it was as if my life as a sound engineer, who owned a recording studio, was no longer what I wanted. My life was in a mess anyway. After burning my fingers a couple of times by working with studios who did not think a person with my condition could perform well, my friend Nikhil Ghia and I had set up our own recording studio, Brahmasonic. It was an exciting time initially and we even got a couple of breaks—including working with Bollywood music directors Vishal- Shekhar, a few Indian rock bands and clients from the advertising world. We had worked with luminaries such as jazz percussionist Trilok Gurtu and produced all of singer and musician Sidd Coutto's solo albums.

But we realized soon that our clients were giving all their good projects to someone else and the inconsequential work to us. We shut Brahmasonic after five years because nobody trusted me with sound engineering due to my condition!

That turned out to be the happiest decision of my life. My soul was shrinking from being in a closed, sound-proof, windowless room all day, and only emerging late in the evening when the sun had already set. I had been struggling in such studio rooms for ten years and for a person who loves being outdoors, that was very depressing. I wanted to do something more interesting with my life. I was obsessed by my rendezvous with the tiger and remember spending entire days and nights in front of a computer, reading up everything I could about them.

The idea came to me one day while I sat watching Animal Planet and I called up my uncle who had first introduced me to the mountains and wilderness, taking me on treks to the Himalayas and to tiny fishing villages in Maharashtra, where he taught me fishing and swimming, and to experience another life. 'How can I get a job saving tigers?' I asked him, half expecting to be laughed at. Instead, he told me that he knew Fateh Singh Rathore, the man who had dedicated his life to the cause of protecting tigers at the Ranthambore Tiger Reserve. I called up Rathore without wasting any time and he told me I could join a wildlife conservation leadership workshop that he was planning soon.

It was just what I wanted. I grabbed the opportunity and two weeks later, without a second thought about what I was getting into, I was in Ranthambore. Rathore, also the brain behind the NGO Tiger Watch, was not convinced I would last there and refused to take the fee in advance, but I told him nothing on earth would make me change my mind. For the next fifteen days, I went on safaris and saw animals and birds, and nature at its best. I was captivated by the possibilities that this life presented.

Opportunities come to people who take the road less travelled. While at Ranthambore, the people at the NGO asked me about myself and when I told them that I was a sound engineer, they happened to mention that many of the poachers operating in the jungle were musicians from the Moghya tribe who played a range of instruments, including bagpipes. I was intrigued and fascinated. As part of their rehabilitation programme, the poachers were being taught some income generating skills, including handicrafts using locally available raw material, but it struck me that it was possible to engage with them more deeply by involving them with their music.

When my course was complete at that camp, I stayed back a couple of days and recorded some of their music to take back to Mumbai with me where I made a couple of my musician friends, including Sid Cuotto, listen to it. It took me a year but I eventually convinced Sid to go to Ranthambore with me a to do a proper recording with the poachers. The sequence of events as they panned out after that is hard to believe. Our tickets to Ranthambore were confirmed and at a party that evening, we ran into Sughandha Garg, an actor and filmmaker friend of ours who heard our story and promptly signed up to go with us! In fact, she woke up her father at midnight and had him book her tickets. It then struck us that another photographer friend, Natasha, could help, too. If we were shooting a film, we might as well do stills, we thought, and got her on board as well.

It was a memorable time shooting with the poachers. Six of them and two kids had gotten together this informal band that performed at community weddings. Part of this group was this extraordinary guy who, in the middle of nowhere, played a bagpipe made out of camel skin and a contraption made out of his shirt, with a pocket still on it! A traditional bagpipe has four pipes, this one had only one pipe, but the basic concept was the same. To see a guy play a bagpipe in the middle of Rajasthan was a strange and unique experience.

We shot them with a Handycam, some of them singing and the others playing their instruments, and decided that we would figure out what to do with the footage once we returned home. We never realized it but after almost a year on the editing table, we had an extraordinary thirty-minute documentary on our hands plus an album of techno-tribal music called *With A Little Help* which was then remixed by different artists!

We made a 1000 DVD copies and gave it to Tiger Watch so that they could sell them and fund their future rehabilitation project for poachers. As I saw it, the rehab project could be a self-sustainable one since the poachers were contributing to it with their music.

That was only the beginning of my tryst with tigers and my love for the jungles. I've spent the last five years on the ground, roaming around in jungles, learning all about wildlife conservation, the reasons why human beings turn poachers, and the uneasy relationship between man and animal, each trying to protect themselves. In 2010 alone, I made nineteen trips to Ranthambore. I have worked as 'tiger tracker and guide' for guests in hotels around wildlife sanctuaries and volunteered in some twenty protected forests for tigers because when you do that, they involve you in a lot of other activities that increases your understanding of the problem.

As I spent more time watching tigers, I started getting an idea of exactly what the tiger is fighting against, just so that it can survive. Their existence is in question all the time. I was restless and wanted to do more in the conservation space. Last year, I got together with a friend, Avantika Chandra, and after a lot of brainstorming, we set up PROWL, a non-profit organization that works towards preservation of wildlife and their habitat. There are thousands of NGOs in India trying to save the tiger, the black bears, rhinos, even cows and goats. But after you save them, you need some place to keep them, too. Our forests are not growing, they're in fact, shrinking. And poaching is a very real problem which will not go away if we don't give poachers alternate income-generating skills. My stint as Community Conservation Officer, where I worked in anti-poaching and rehabilitation of poachers, have helped me hugely in understanding the root cause of the problem.

At PROWL, we do a range of activities that are designed to bring the problem to the discussion table and find viable solutions for it. We have tiger awareness camps and work with former poachers, some of whom now help us at our organization. Months into our initiative we realized that NGOs need to be self-sustaining and that took us to a whole new journey, On The Prowl, a new venture where I take nature and wildlife enthusiasts into the jungles, mountains, and on nature trails to teach them the art of wildlife photography, for a fee. A few years ago, I myself, took off to the Masai Mara National Reserve, in Kenya, where I learnt wildlife photography at a workshop conducted by Nature Wanderers, National Geographic, and Canon. Plus, I have a diploma course in photography and that has proved to be a valuable experience for On The Prowl. When I take my students into the jungles, I get some priceless opportunity to catch tigers in the wild. I have loads of these photographs and eventually plan to put them up for sale in order to fund future projects for PROWL. A part of our profit from these expeditions will go to various NGOs working in wildlife conservation and that in itself is a great motivator for us.

In December 2013, Prowl teamed up with Saving Tiger and Conservation Consortium India (CCI) to conduct a unique First Aid and Outdoor Survival training for 150 forest guards at the Sundarban Tiger Reserve. The Sundarbans has a very treacherous terrain and a majority of the tigers in the reserve are confirmed man eaters. They're very aggressive and a lot of forest guards are attacked by tigers. The guards have no idea about survival training nor do they know what first aid means. And when you're working outdoors, in the jungle from morning till evening in harsh conditions, this knowledge could be the difference between life and death.

We knew we did not have the money to take up an ambitious project of this kind but we used our combined network of friends and ran a fund raiser on Facebook to distribute first aid kits to 150 Forest guards in the Sunderban Tiger Reserve. Each of the kits cost Rs 600 and thankfully for us, our Facebook friends contributed generously so we were able to raise Rs 1.50 lakhs the first time. Enthused by the support, we are now planning to extend the project to other reserves as well.

There have been other small steps too. Impressed with my conservation efforts, a firm, Gibson Guitars, sponsored Prowl's project to get a ten-foot guitar painted live at Mumbai's famed Kala Ghoda festival to create awareness about tigers.

When I look back at my life now, I find it unbelievably amusing and a bit amazing that I never walked till as late as 5 years of age but spend my time today criss-crossing the country's wildlife sanctuaries, tracking tigers, and roaming around in the wild with scores of people following me with bated breath. I have lived in jungles, climbed mountains, enjoyed the soul-stirring beauty of the Himalayas, and come face to face with tigers on many occasions. And each time, instead of the raw fear that people experience when they see one, my heart leaps with joy and my determination to spend my time in their company only strengthens further.

To this day, I remember the Himalayan treks that I was introduced to by my uncle. From Manali, we would walk up to the start of the river Beas. I've also done one Indo-British camp where we walked from Rohtang pass to Chandratal. It was a six-day trek one way. We went to this lake in Chandratal, 14,500 feet up, camped there overnight, and walked back. It was easily one of the most beautiful things I have ever done in my life. I have done fourteen days of non-stop walking in the Himalayas, in the middle of nowhere. That's when you hear true silence and come to understand its meaning. In the urban jungle of city life, you feel like you're the king, but when you are standing surrounded by the Himalayas, you feel so small. It puts so much into perspective.

When I grew up, I started going into the outdoors on my

own. There have been times when I would get myself a train ticket and take off for fifteen-days or a month. Often, I head to the jungle, or the Himalayas, and do nothing at all but wake up in the morning, look at the mountains, go down for a small walk to the river, and sit there enjoying my own company. My mother is used to it now and so are my friends.

So often, I've woken up, called a friend, and we have taken a car and gone on a road trip, deciding where to go as we drive along. We drive and camp where we please and the freedom that it gives is so good even though it sometimes gets us into a spot with wild animals.

At a camp near Solang in the Himalayas, I went out one day to relieve myself and I suddenly heard the rustling of leaves from somewhere above me. I peeped from behind the rock I was sitting near and was frightened out of my skin when I saw a huge Himalayan black bear coming down the mountain. Luckily I was behind a rock, so he couldn't see me and did not sniff out my presence. I sat there praying for ten minutes flat after that incident!

There have been other interesting encounters of the wild kind and each time I have learnt something from it. Like the time I along with a couple of wildlife enthusiasts and conservationists and got stalked by three tigers at the Corbett National Park in December 2010.

When the then Deputy Field Officer of the park heard that we were there, he asked to meet us. He was, at that time, seeking various ways to reduce the pressure of tourists in the main Corbett area and wanted us to go there and tell him what animals and birds were to be found at the Sitabani forest area, which was not open to tourists. Our jaws fell at this unexpected opportunity and before he could change his mind, we had said yes to the proposition. There are no roads in Sitabani and we would have to walk all the way there, but to get to walk officially in a tiger reserve was like a dream come true for us.

We stayed that night in the government guest house and were off like heroes early in the morning. There is a temple in the forest that is dedicated to Sita. Legend goes that she lived there after Ram abandoned her after her abduction by Ravan and her return from Lanka. We explored that for a bit and set out, walking along a mountain stream to get on our task. Since it was unknown territory, we felt safe following the stream. There was a bank of sand followed by a short curtain of grass, and then the stream. This gave us a feeling of security because if there was any danger or wild animal approaching, we'd be able to see it from far. After walking for 45 minutes to an hour, we noticed our first pug mark on the river bed. We knew immediately that it was a big female tiger. And since the entire sand on the bank except the pug mark was dry, we knew she had crossed over from the other side of the river a few minutes ago. We presumed she had gone into the jungle but five minutes later, we saw a second pugmark, this time heading in the opposite direction. Dealing with two tigers is a scary proposition and suddenly, we felt very, very worried. Just as we were getting over that shock, we heard a low growling from the bushes and knew that a big cat was watching us from behind the bank of bushes. We froze for a moment but decided to proceed, with three of us looking in either direction so that we would not be ambushed by one of the tigers. I am sure you have heard the phrase 'When it rains, it pours'. We had only proceeded a few metres ahead when one of the team members stopped dead in his tracks, pointing towards the hill and there he was, a magnificent big cat, walking up the hill. That would have been okay, but suddenly the cat stopped and turned to directly look at us, emitting a menacing snarl. We ignored that, too, and started walking ahead, our hearts in our mouth but there, in front of us, was another tiger, walking directly towards us! He was still a distance away and we ran that day like never before to save our lives. Tigers can't climb trees because they're too heavy. I don't know how I climbed that tree, but for the next three months, muscles I didn't know existed hurt. For the next three hours we sat on the tree waiting for the tigers to leave. Thankfully, they went off without any fuss.

Even after that incident, I continued to go on walks with forest guards in Ranthambore and the thing I have learnt is that a tiger will never attack you face front. He will only attack from the side or back. So if you're ever walking and see a tiger in front of you, no matter how big the tiger is, the best thing to do is to continue walking in his direction and 99 percent of the time, he'll go into the bush and walk around you, in order to avoid you. They don't want to have a face to face confrontation with humans. You just keep alert and continue walking.

From being a boy who could hardly walk without balance because of cerebral palsy to being a tiger monitoring expert, a naturalist, and a lecturer on wildlife all over the country, my life has been an adventure through and through. Most young people—including me at some point in my earlier life—worry about earning a decent livelihood and getting all the trappings of an urban life. But living in the jungles and waking up to the call of a tiger, a deer, or the sound of peacocks is altogether different. My dream now, is to be able to live in a jungle. I've learnt that if you follow your heart, things work out in the end. Following a tiger's trail is my calling…

Jqved Abidi

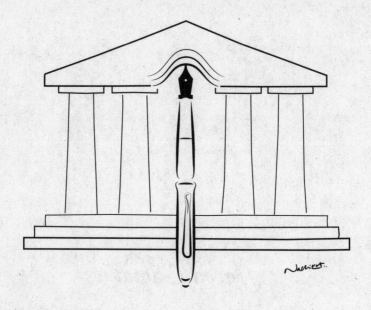

Javed has been conceptualized as a fountain pen, given his credentials as a journalist, as a man who believes that change can happen by drafting policies and framing appropriate laws and being a classy old-timer. But the fountain pen does not exist in isolation. It, in fact, stands out as a central pillar and creates a gentle curve in the middle of rigid, solid, and heavy straight lines. The curve is really the much-needed cure and a change…and the structure is the establishment itself, and its mindset. The depiction also brings about the long, patient, and dignified battle that Javed has fought almost single-handedly to bring about this desirable dent to the forefront.

The story of Javed Abidi's life is the kind that Hollywood films are made of. There is pathos, drama, action, and resolution, and there is a protagonist whose spirit is indefatigable. Being confined to a wheelchair at the age of 15 due to a congenital condition did not deter the young man from pushing his boundaries. In fact, he seems to know no boundaries. From the by-lanes of the university town of Aligarh in Uttar Pradesh to life on a university campus in the Unites States to becoming a popular journalist who used unconventional way to land a story to starting a momentous campaign for the rights of people with disability, his life is the stuff that could inspire the most hardened among us.

Abidi has a reputation of being a serious sort of man with whom you can't make small conversation and I was nervous as I waited for him in the tiny office room in Delhi that is replete with images of his relentless campaign for disability rights. When he wheels himself in, it is evident he is suffering from a bad bout of cold, but all of that disappears as I lead him on a journey down memory lane and he recounts his fascinating story from his hometown in Uttar Pradesh to the relentless action that he is now involved in, as Executive Director of the National Centre For Promotion of Employment For People With Disability (NCPEPD)—an advocacy group for people with disabilities that has an iconic status in the country.

I was born in the university town of Aligarh where my father was a lecturer at the Aligarh Muslim University. The first thing the doctors noticed when I was born was a lump on my lower back and in their own wisdom, they pronounced that I would not live beyond forty days. My parents were crushed. I was their first born and they were looking forward to raising me. My father decided to hoodwink destiny by naming me Javed which means immortal in Arabic. The joke in my family now is that my father's plan worked: It has been more than forty years and I'm still around.

In a way, this also defines who I am: I'm not one who easily gives up, I don't accept defeats. We all suffer setbacks, but I'm like the plastic toy that you keep slapping down but it always keeps coming right up again.

Our life was simple. We were a small nuclear family and I led a normal, middle-class life with a younger brother and sister. The lump on my back turned out to be a congenital condition called Spina Bifida (It is caused by the incomplete closing of the embryonic neural tube.) but when my parents took me to doctors in Delhi, they were advised to not interfere with it, if I was growing normally. Then, at the age of 8, I started dragging my right leg while walking and the doctors decided it was time to operate on me. Only, moments into the surgery at AIIMS, they realized that they had goofed up with their delay. The lump had grown and it had affected my nerves, and they knew that my life would be complicated from there on. When I came out of surgery, I was worse than I was before. I was limping and gradually my condition deteriorated till at the age of 10 I had to start using crutches, and take to the wheelchair at 15.

But none of this made my parents falter even for a moment. My father made sure that he gave me as normal a childhood as possible, sending me to a regular school, sparing no efforts to give me the best education possible. He supplemented his income by giving tuitions in the evening after work so that he could look after my needs, considering my disability. Life went on as usual and one day, I found myself ready to enter university.

It is then that I realized that school was like the proverbial well where everything was safe and secure for the frogs within its walls. In school, you don't feel your disability so much because you are in the classroom all day and the teachers have to come in to teach. University was a huge jungle where I had to go up a number of flights of stairs to get to my various classrooms. It was difficult, formidable at times, but I learnt to cope. I was also lucky that I had a good set of friends who would pick up my wheelchair and carry me everywhere so that I never really felt 'handicapped' at any point in my life. I've heard horror stories from people about how they were teased or how they had bad experiences. But in my life, I don't recall any such incident, maybe because I lived in a small town where everyone knew everyone. Or maybe I was just plain lucky. Whatever the reasons were, I was very comfortable with my own disability. I never really felt disabled because I was able to do everything I wanted to do—roam around, go to the movies, and hang out with my friends.

In the 80s, it was always the father who decided what their children should do with their life. Mine wanted me to be a doctor. In those days, sons had to become either engineers or doctors, so I, too, went through a few years of torture, learning biology and chemistry, but I hated every moment of it. I was more into debates and extra-curricular activities, and when my father left the university to go to Delhi to become Joint Secretary of the Congress Party at Mrs Indira Gandhi's insistence (he was an admirer and follower of Jawaharlal Nehru), I decided to follow my own calling, albeit secretly. My father was a loving, caring man, but he was also very strict. So, the years after he shifted to Delhi was when the process of my own self-discovery began. The first thing I did was to not appear for my medical exams and the second was to sign up for a Bachelor of Arts degree. I knew that writing, reading, and debates were the kind of things that attracted me. I chose English Literature because that was my father's subject and I had grown up hearing him lecturing on Milton and Shakespeare. I studied Political Science and Linguistics as well and I happily moved from being a potential medical student to a potential nothing student. When he came to know, this broke my father's heart and he just gave up on me, slotting me as a no-gooder. The irony was that I was doing pretty well in my life, getting elected to positions, winning trophies for the university, and getting invited to important events. Even the vice chancellor of the university knew me!

A chance meeting with an American acquaintance of my

father took my life in an altogether different direction. This friend took a fondness for me and over long conversations, he told me I would be able to explore my full potential at universities in America. He told me life was different for people with disabilities in that country and eventually, he helped me apply to a few colleges in the US. When I got admitted to a couple of them though, all hell broke loose. My father thought I was throwing away my life in futile things but eventually, he calmed down and even managed to find some funding for my course there. I landed in the US in 1985 and it was a whole new world for me. Of course, there were the usual cultural shocks and the newness of living on my own for the first time ever but what impacted me the most was that, every nook and corner of the university campus—from the living areas to the classrooms to the library, gymnasium and even the football field—was completely accessible to people with disabilities. From the university campus, I could get into a bus and go downtown to roam around freely. A large number of students with disabilities were on campus and I saw they lived an equal life. It was while I was in the university there that I realized I wanted to be a journalist so I did my degree in mass communication and started writing for my university's newspaper regularly.

Those four or five years at the university were, I think, the best years of my life. I was the President of the India Club, President of the International Students' Union, and participated actively in campus politics, getting elected as the representative of my college to the students' union. But when I graduated in 1989, I decided to come back to India. By that time, my entire family had moved to Delhi. We had a home there but my father thought it was a foolish move on my part because he insisted that I would never get the same opportunities that I had in the US. I, on the other hand, thought that with my qualifications and my degree, editors would line up to employ me. It was the rudest shock to me when I spent the six months after my arrival in Delhi, searching for a job in journalism. I went from newspaper to newspaper, magazine to magazine, meeting editors, and they all patted me on the back, telling me how brave and intelligent I was. But nobody gave me a job because they were all looking at my wheelchair and presuming that I could never be a journalist because, as they put it, 'How could I chase a story?' Not one of them was ready to give me a chance and, for the first time in my life, I felt as if I was 'handicapped'.

Since I don't give up easily, I decided to scale down my ambition and thankfully, there was a small city magazine which was doing an election story and had run into some difficulty with it. They wanted to do interviews with the members of parliament from the seven constituencies of Delhi and were finding it hard to get time with the three remaining ones—Jagdish Tytler, H.K.L. Bhagat, and K.C. Pant. Because it was a small magazine, none of these heavy weights wanted to give them an interview.

I volunteered and managed to swing interviews with both Tytler and Bhagat and, suddenly, the magazine started looking at me with a fresh eye. That left K.C. Pant on my list. I believe that luck plays an important role in everyone's life. Sometimes all your credentials won't help if you don't have luck by your side. One morning, I was reading the gossip column of a newspaper and it said there that the son of K.C. Pant, the then defence minister, was arriving that day from the US, to get married. I planned a scheme in my head. I called for a rented car, asking them to send me a brand new ambassador car so that when I arrived at the gate of Pant's residence, no one would stop the gleaming car or question us. Getting out of the car on to my wheelchair, the guards looked at me curiously but I went up to them and confidently pulled out an identity card and gave it to them. It was actually my social security card from the US. Overwhelmed by the aura of importance that I displayed, they presumed that I was the son's friend and let me in without a word or even a cursory cross-check. No question asked, no answer given, no lies spoken, and I managed to break into the home of the then Defence Minister of India. Now that's what I call luck.

What followed was unbelievable. I headed towards the verandah where there were a lot of people already waiting to meet the minister. When the door opened and Pant came out, the waiting crowd rushed towards him. I, too, thrust my micro-recorder, asked him a few questions and he answered them, without once asking me as to who I was or which media organization I represented. And just like that, I had my interview and the people at the magazine were amazed at how I had swung it. That was the turning point of my career in journalism and I became the toast of the publication in no time at all.

I've used this example in my conversations with people with disability. It does not matter that you are a person with disability. What matters is your attitude, your determination to go after your goal, and be firm with your resolve. Can you imagine a person on a wheelchair breaking into the house of the defence minister of India? I did that because I was confident about my abilities and was determined to interview him!

After that interview, I became the go-to person for every difficult story because they knew I would get it by hook or crook. In the months that followed, I got some plum assignments and managed to meet some top celebrities, including Amitabh Bachchan. In about six months, I was writing for some of the top newspapers and magazines of India, including the *Times of India* and *Illustrated Weekly*. I was among the first journalists to meet Chandrasekhar when he took over as the prime minister and soon, I was being noticed by editors and was hosting a youth show on Doordarshan. Life was like a dream.

It was then that the next twist in my tale happened. My father was a Congress party person who worked closely with Mrs Indira Gandhi and Mr Rajiv Gandhi. After Rajiv's death, my father was shaken very badly because he was very fond of him. He sought an appointment from the family to go and meet Mrs Sonia Gandhi who was just beginning to meet people after the mourning period. While we were there, we got talking casually and the conversation veered towards disability, maybe because I was on a wheelchair. A few days later, she called me for another meeting and asked me then if I knew that she was setting up the Rajiv Gandhi Foundation. I had heard about it, I told her, and she told me to go and meet Mr Wajahat Habibullah. I thought they would offer me a mid-level official's job but I was astonished when he asked if I would be interested in setting up the disabilities unit of the foundation. It was early 1992 and I was just 26 years old, enjoying my stint as a journalist, and this put huge dilemma on my plate. He said I could think about it for a week before arriving at a decision. I could clearly see I was being given an opportunity of a lifetime, a huge platform from where I could address issues facing the disabled that had bothered me till then, whether it was my own experiences with discrimination and being denied a job or all the inaccessibility I saw around me while travelling.

On the other hand, I knew that if I take that up, then I'd have to give up journalism, my passion and for which I had worked so hard.

But one week later, I decided that I would join the foundation, my decision based on the simple premise that one journalist less would not make any difference whatsoever to journalism in India whereas one more person working in the disability movement would, perhaps, add strength to the cause. It was May 1992. I had no brief for my position at the Rajiv Gandhi Foundation but my job was to advise them on what I thought they should do for people with disability. And the very first thing we did was to look around the country to see what was happening in this space, and we realized there was a lot of service delivery going on for the disabled but unfortunately, it was a lot of charity, driven by pity. Many NGOs were running special schools or giving vocational training but those training courses were teaching the disabled stuff like making candles or envelopes and diyas. Who would ever get a job after this kind of vocational training?

We realized that there was no law on the rights of people with disabilities. That was the beginning of a journey of many years during which, among other things, we set up a school for children with developmental disabilities in the Kalahandi district in Odisha and reactivated the Lifeline Express, a train that housed a mobile hospital where corrective surgeries for polio, cataract, and deafness were undertaken in the remotest corners of the country. But we realized soon enough that the train could go on forever doing the surgeries and we would not have touched even a fraction of the disabled population in our country. We realized that what we needed most was a comprehensive national policy framework for the disabled in India.

That is when we pushed the government of India to start working towards the law. That Mrs Gandhi was our chairperson helped the cause of the disabled hugely, especially with the Congress government. In less than three years, between 1992 and 1995, we were able to put together a law, take it to the parliament, and get it passed. I was just 30 years old and there was a huge sense of achievement about this milestone. To put it in perspective, the Persons with Disabilities Act, 1995, was the very first law on the rights of people with disabilities in the history of India. There were small policies during the tenure of Mrs Indira Gandhi as PM. For instance, after the Bangladesh war in 1971 she gave a 3 percent reservation to people with disabilities in government jobs. Unfortunately, when it was implemented by the policy makers, it said these jobs would only be in the C and D category, which was the bottom of the pile. Did it then mean that people with disability could only be gardeners or peons and not officers and people in positions of influence?

The 1995 law on the other hand, said there would be a

3 percent reservation across all levels of government jobs, for the disabled. It also gave a 3 percent reservation to disabled students approaching educational institutions in universities, colleges, IITs, and IIMs. Till 1995, there was not a single disabled student in any IIT, IIM, or in any professional college across India. So this was indeed a path breaking, revolutionary law for that time.

The Rajiv Gandhi Foundation platform gave me the opportunity to get to know a very large number of people in a very short time. I travelled to the deepest pockets of the country and met with disabled people, their parents, teachers, professionals, and NGOs, to be able to understand the conditions. The foundation gave a lot of inputs to the technocrats who drafted the law and the law was passed in the winter session of the parliament. Along the way we realized that India did not have a census of the number of people with disability. Till the mid-90s, nobody knew the population of disabled people in India. The only figure the government had was based on the national sample survey, and that said, the population was less than 1 percent.

That is when I came up with the theory that disabled people were an 'invisible minority' in India even though we were a sizeable minority representing 5-6 percent of the country's population. We were invisible because one did not see too many disabled people in colleges, universities, cinema halls, railway stations, or airports. The only few disabled people that one got to see were the beggars at the traffic signals who symbolized the attitude towards the disabled: pity and charity. It was then that we also coined the phrase, 'Movement away from charity to rights', a campaign that we later extended to say that disability was a human rights issue. That was a transformative era for the disabled people in India.

I served in the Rajiv Gandhi Foundation from 1992 to 1997, by when the law had made it possible to provide employment for the disabled, in the public sector but there was still no provision for them in the private sector, which was developing at a fast pace. Then we came up with the idea of an organization which would focus on providing employment opportunities for disabled people in the private sector by collaborating with them, motivating them, and also acting as a watchdog. That was how the National Centre for Promotion of Employment for Disabled People (NCPEDP) was conceived.

NCPEDP was set up in 1996 as a separate organization which received funding from the foundation for two years and was then allowed to grow independently. Mrs Gandhi was so committed to it that she agreed to be the first chairperson of this organization. I was also one of the founding trustees at that time but in 1997, I took over as the Executive Director. It has been a long and tumultuous seventeen years, full of tough battles, victories, and some setbacks, but it has been more than worth all of the difficulties. Much of the work we have undertaken in this period has been with identifying gaps in the policy framework and putting policies in place that gave rights to people with disabilities in this country.

We grew the NCPEDP by forging relationships with government officials, business leaders, and disability groups in various corners of the country. At each stage, they have played a crucial role in what has been achieved for the disabilities sector. It was necessary to keep ourselves focussed so we decided to make December 3—United Nations' International Day of Persons with Disabilities—as the day we would celebrate the success of people with disability and also to build our agenda for future action. The NCPEDP Helen Keller Award, given to individuals and organizations in recognition of their contribution to the advancement of people with disability, is a source of joy not just for me but for all those who work in the sector.

The 1995 law, meanwhile, had been rendered redundant in fifteen years. We lobbied with the UPA government, pointing out that it was an archaic law that had nothing for people with disabilities given the current realities in the country.

It took seven months for the minister to be convinced, after which, a committee was appointed to study and make a new draft and they took two years to do that. The government then took another year to add its own touches to the draft and from there, it went to various ministries and other states for consultation. The new disability bill is now pending before the cabinet and once it gets approval, it will go to the parliament.

The NCPEDP is in the thick of the process—right from being a part of the committees, to submitting papers, to holding consultations across the country, increasing our own knowledge base, and arguing things as forcefully as humanly possible. But even then, sometimes it works, and sometimes it doesn't. India was the 7th country to ratify the UN Convention on the Rights of Persons with Disabilities, one of the first significant countries, and it now has an international obligation. But it is still necessary to have our policies spelt out clearly in our own statutes so that it is airtight. Besides, umbrella laws and policies are good only up to a point, after which it is necessary to examine what is happening on the ground level in implementation in various departments/ministries. Until now, we have identified a total of sixteen ministries that we feel have a direct impact on a disabled person's life and we have started working with them to make them aware of the policies that they would need to put in place for people with disability. Genuine change will only come from laws and policies, not sensitization seminars, poster campaigns, or high-brow conferences.

India is at a very nascent stage when it comes to the rights of people with disability. We have just barely begun to look at disability with the seriousness that it deserves and my only wish right now is the passage of the new disability law. We need at least 50–60 policies that will make it even seem like we genuinely wish to improve things for people with disability in this country.

I remember the struggle that we underwent to simply get the government to include people with disability in our census. As all our census reports till 1990 never even mentioned or acknowledged the existence of people with disability, we wrote to the census commission in 1998, requesting them to include this segment when the next census came around in 2001. I was aghast when I received a reply saying that they would not include a question about disabled people in the census. In 2000, we declared war and took to the streets in a concerted manner for six months, voicing our demands.

It soon turned into a huge national issue. Editorials were written, rallies were held, and the matter went right up to the Home Minister L.K. Advani, under whose purview the census fell. And then, one fine day, the matter was resolved just about the time when the census questionnaire was about to go for printing. The government finally agreed to acknowledge that disabled people existed and needed to be counted in the census, too!

That was one of the biggest victories of the disability movement. When the 2001 census figures were released, it said that 2.1 percent of the population of India was disabled. That totalled up to a staggering number of 21 million disabled people, if not more. For us, the numbers were low. We finally believed that at least 5–6 percent of India's population was affected by one disability or another, and the counting hand not included all of them.

However, the government could no longer pretend that this segment of our populace did not exist. Things started moving fast: the planning commission started looking at disability with a new eye as opposed to the first ten five-year plans when there was almost no mention of disability! The finance ministry started allocating more resources to making India's public spaces and railway stations accessible to the disabled. Even then, it will take decades to complete the process. It was only after a sustained battle that the issue of disability got significant attention in the 11th and 12th five-year plans and as a result of our battles, significantly higher resources have been allocated for people with disability.

We realize today that it is not the best thing that every decision regarding people with disability has to be taken by the Ministry of Social Justice because, by itself, the ministry will not be able to resolve all the problems of the disabled people of

India. These can only be addressed at the ministries concerning those particular subjects. For instance, if a matter has to do with universities and colleges of India, the HRD ministry should tackle it. We have been saying all along that disability is a cross cutting issue, but in real life, or in governance, it is still not being made a cross cutting issue. So, we now want to devote the next few years to getting this policy gap addressed, even though it is easier said than done.

None of what I have done or achieved over the years has been planned. I could never have imagined that I'd get to the US from my middle-class family in Aligarh, that I would transform into a 4.0 GPA student there, or that I would return home when a world of opportunities was open for me in America. I could never imagine that I would join the Rajiv Gandhi Foundation and that my work would take me on an extraordinary and intense mission that would become my life itself. I believe that we are presented with twists and turns throughout our life and the only thing we can do is to do the best we can, at that point in time. Sometimes, I cannot believe the story of my own life and I am surprised that I've come so far, and have done the kind of things I have done. Sometimes, when I attend public functions or address large rallies, people come up to me and congratulate me, and tell me that I inspire them. At such moments, I feel like there are two different people inside me. The small-town boy who wanted to be a journalist and the one who has become a well-known activist for disability rights. From watching my father's life, seeing how powerful he was at one time and how all of that slipped away, and left him helpless towards the end of his life, I have learnt that none of this matters. I am convinced that there are different phases in our life and all of them are temporary, so it doesn't bother me beyond a point.

What you do need is to have the courage of your conviction. To say what is to be said. And to do that, you need to have freedom of speech. NCPEDP does not take a single rupee in funding from the government, so we are free to vocalize our demands and point out stuff that others who are beholden to the government cannot point out. Nor do we take money from anyone else who will then limit our freedom of speech.

For me, every day is a new day and each day brings with it a new challenge. Even today, I feel the same enthusiasm, the same vigour, and the same excitement towards my work that I felt twenty years ago. The challenges, the targets, the people around you, and the times keep changing and you have to adapt yourself. In a very humble way, I feel good that I have been able to contribute and bring about some change. At the same time I do realize that I've not been able to do as much as I had wanted or could have done. There is still so much left to do.

What drives me each day is the desire to bring about as much change as possible in as little time. We have fifty years of catching up to do in the disability space and we really need to hurry up because India cannot possibly wait that long. The disabled persons of my generation have paid the price for the lackadaisical attitude of our forefathers, but what we are doing now is for the future generations. Already, we can see the difference. Over a thousand students with disability study in Delhi University alone. Our IITs, IIMs, and all our top professional colleges have now opened up and that is a sign that change is happening and is inevitable. People with disability now occupy leadership positions across sectors. For me, the biggest sign of change is the fact that disabled people are now holding positions in the civil services, something that was unimaginable a few years ago. In fact, from the first batch who entered the civil services about ten years ago, some already are district magistrates. And these are boys and girls who are going to become secretaries and joint secretaries, and ambassadors of our country tomorrow. It is my hope that once they are in power positions, they will not forget who they are; they will not forget their disability identity.

Malathi Holla

A medal of glory is the equivalence used for bringing out the personality of Malathi Holla. A collection of 300-plus medals will leave a permanent trace of Malathi in this world. The medal has a spiral enclosed within... an ancient symbol that holds multiple meanings such as, a sacred journey, consciousness, all-encompassing universality, and in a more subtle manner, the wheel of her chariot, rotating swiftly in the races! Malathi says, 'I wish I could fly like a bird fearlessly from one place to another.' Therefore, the ribbon of the medal has been stylized like the wings, depicting the fact that Malathi has indeed flown high in the sky and gone places flapping her wings, and carrying the torch of glory, that kindles the mind!

I am late for my evening appointment with Malathi Holla at a coffee shop near Bengaluru's Kanteerava Stadium. When I walk in, she is taking the staff to task because they have failed to provide a ramp outside the café in order to make it accessible to disabled customers, despite several representations by her.

Malathi Holla might have spent the better part of her life on a wheelchair but she is a woman with a formidable willpower that has taken her to far corners of the world, representing India at various sports events—including the Paralympics, the Asian and Commonwealth Games, and the World Masters—where she has picked up an astounding 300-plus medals! Malathi is also the proud recipient of the coveted Arjuna and Padma Shri Awards and is known among sporting circles as the 'Champion of Champions'.

But none of this makes her a satisfied soul. Each day, she says, she finds something else that remains to be done, so she can give back to the society that helped make a little girl on a wheelchair into a role model that many aspire to follow and learn from. It is rare in our country to find people with disability occupying positions of responsibility at the workplace, even though there are a handful of employers who are catalyzing a change in this space. Malathi herself works as a manager with

Syndicate Bank in Bengaluru, but her bigger responsibility is the twenty children with disability that she nurtures at Mathru Foundation, a charitable trust that she set up with a few friends.

'When I was a child , I wanted to be first among my friends who used to run to the backyard to pick the mangoes that had fallen off trees. I wanted to fly like a bird fearlessly from one place to another. But as I grew up, I realized that you need legs to run and wings to fly. I was hurt, but I didn't give up. I knew, one day, I would run... Thus, I took up sports and decided to do something different in life. Yes, we are different and even our lives should be a shining example of that difference,' she says in her autobiography, *A Different Spirit*.

I was born in 1958 as a very normal child to my parents who hailed from a small village near Udipi, and we were very, very poor.

My mother used to tell me that I started walking and even running when I was 9-months-old. I was naughty, and it was very difficult for them to handle me. When I was about 14 months old, I got a raging fever that was, in fact, a polio attack that left me paralyzed neck down. Till I was 5-years-old, the only portion of my body that could move was my neck.

With four children to feed and no prospects, my parents migrated to Bengaluru so that my father could work at his cousin's Udipi hotel. Since he was illiterate, he was happy that he could find any employment at all. My mother took on the responsibility of making sure that I, her youngest born, could get some chance in life and so, every afternoon, she would put me on her hip and we would take the bus to the Victoria hospital at the other end of the city so that I could get the electric shock treatment which, she was told, would help me regain some strength in my limbs. It was four hours of treatment every day and she would stand beside me when I screamed from the pain as the electrical shock tore through my body.

This went on for two years till one day, miraculously, I regained control and strength in my upper body.

When I was about 5 years old, doctors at the hospital told my parents that I stood a better chance if they admitted me to the Ishwari Prasad Dattatraya Orthopaedic Centre in Chennai where I could get boarding, lodging, medical treatment, and education, under one roof. The centre worked with physically challenged children not just to help them become more independent physically but also rehabilitate them with life and livelihood skills. It was a tough decision for my parents, but they wanted my life to be better and so I lived there for the next fifteen years of my life, growing up with 100-150 children with various degrees of disability. It was hard because I missed my siblings and my parents but my natural aptitude to make friends soon had me bonding with the other children at the centre.

I was a naughty child, completely undisciplined and yet, nothing happened at that centre without me—neither sports nor extracurricular activities—because I was good at all of this. I played the tabla, the violin, and participated in various music and dance programs. It was an institution for learning that gave me a new life by attending to my pain and giving me happiness. I never took my life at the centre as a struggle or challenge. I think that if I had been raised in my own house by my family, I would have been happy but would have never got the experiences and the learning that I got at the centre.

In some ways, I think the stay there gave me the life I live today. If I wallowed in pity in my earlier life, the sight of so many children in far worse conditions than me, woke me up to my blessings. Faced with pain and suffering of those children, I quickly assumed the role of a friend and caretaker, helping them out with their chores that often included attending to their personal hygiene. The centre had very limited staff and it was not always possible for them to give 100 percent attention to each of us. I, myself, was at that point crawling on the ground to get around but that did not stop my heart from going out to another soul who was in need.

I felt the first stirring of compassion in those years at the centre and soon, I was a friend and companion to many of the co-boarders. Living with so many kids who were disabled in different ways, I learnt to look after everybody's interests, often taking up the weaker one's cause, even if my opponent was a formidable one. To this day, I cannot stand anyone cheating or bullying a weaker person and I cannot help but go and take bullies to task. Those fifteen years at the centre, away from my family, made me grow up early and pick up leadership qualities.

During my stay there, I noticed there were children whose parents never came to meet them. They washed their hands off any further responsibility of their children with the result that those kids even spent their summer holidays alone at the centre when the rest of us went home to be with our family. I made sure that when I returned from my own stay with my family, I carried lots of delicious homemade goodies that I shared with them.

My father meant everything to me—all through my stay at the institute and till his death. He was the one who believed in me and stood by me when I went through surgery after surgery to correct my limbs at the Chennai centre. My mother hardly ever came to visit me because she could not bear the sight of my surgery-ravaged body. She had seen me in pain as a kid and she could not take any more of my pain. Besides, the sight of so many children with so many challenges disturbed her. My siblings were constant sources of love and support in those years and would await my arrival home on vacations so that they could pamper and spoil me with their love.

It was my father's dream that I go to college and get myself a good education. After fifteen long years at the Chennai centre, I returned home and under his guidance, I enrolled for my junior college at the Maharani College. My elation at this feat was soon dampened when I found it very challenging to get to my second floor classroom every day. In tears, I told my father I was dropping out but he stood his ground, telling me I would have to go back to college and talk to them about the issue. 'You only get what you ask for in life. If you don't ask, chances are no one will know what you need and so, they can never give you what you want,' he said. The next day, I told the principal about my situation, expecting a cold, unhelpful response but to my utter surprise, the very next day, the college decided to shift the classroom to the lower level so that I could attend my classes!

That bit of advice has stayed with me and proved to be a priceless lesson through all these years. Every time I have felt that I am being overlooked or being denied something that is rightfully mine, I have dug my foot in and asked for my right. In 1979, when the government of India made a rule that barred all differently-abled sportspersons from being even considered for the Arjuna awards, it made me very angry. Physically challenged people have to work doubly hard to get anything in life even though we put ourselves through the most daunting physical and mental challenges to bring laurels to our country. I found

134

it very unfair and did not think twice before challenging the preposterous rule. It took a lot out of me to stand up against the powers that were but when I won, it was a victory for not just me, but all the differently-abled people in this country. Decades later, when my name was announced as an Arjuna award recipient in 1995, it was time for a second celebration—I had proved my point beyond doubt!

I have come a long way since those days when a flight of stairs seemed a formidable challenge to me. What has helped me along the way was the fact that I discovered the therapeutic value of sports, a world where I could escape the pain of my everyday life. In the decades since my college days, I have become a wheelchair athlete of repute, a Paralympian who is known all over the world. When people tell me they look upon me as an inspirational , motivational figure, I think of all the struggles along the way, the mind-numbing pain, the cynicism, the indifference of society, as I struggled to make a niche for myself. Not many would believe it today if I said that I earned most of the 300 national and international awards in my kitty using a borrowed wheelchair. That was how hard the struggle was.

My connection with sports began at the centre in Chennai where we were encouraged to be physically active so that we could build up our strength and endurance. I loved participating in the sports competitions held on 3rd December, the United Nations' International Day for People with Disabilities. Back in Bengaluru in 1975, after my 15-year stay at Chennai, I had the opportunity to participate in the first ever national sports event for the disabled, organized by the National Society for

Equal Opportunities for the Handicapped (NASEOH). I never imagined that the two precious gold and silver medals that I won in that event would lead me into a lifelong relationship with athletics and sports, and would change my equation with the world. After years of competing in national events—once even winning a 100-metre track event against men, when there were no other women competitors—I got the chance to participate in the 1988 Paralympics in South Korea. It was both exhilarating and disheartening. While I had the chance to go for an international event, I realized, at once, how difficult it was to win there. Disabled sportsmen in India don't even get coaches and have to learn everything on their own. I stood no chance against the competitors who had clear-cut strategies and techniques. In addition, I realized I would have to hire a special kind of wheelchair to participate in the track events meaningfully. I had only days to do that and, not surprisingly, I did not win any medal there. But I did manage to finish the 200-metre race in 56:10 seconds, a record that no Indian female athlete in this category has bettered till date.

Afterwards, it was as if a new world had opened up for me. At the World Masters Games at Denmark in 1989, I swept away four gold medals in two track events, plus javelin and shot put. Eventually, I decided against participating in track events because I simply could not afford to rent a wheelchair at exorbitant prices.

The 1994 Asian Games at Beijing, China, were a memorable experience. I had never dreamt my sporting career would grow so big. I put my heart and soul into training for the event at Pune where I had retreated. The fruit of my labour was a silver medal

Aisha—A smile is the answer to any problem in life

The family that has fun together stays together

Her best friend

Ankit with family

Ankit—looking forward to a brilliant future

Receiving the Hellen Keller award was a proud moment

Friends for life. Ashwin with constant companion, Bharat

Ashwin

George Abraham

George Abraham with family

Girisha showing off his silver medal at the paralympics, 2012

Reaching for the sky. 'I want the gold at Rio...'

Exulting in the after glow of his silver medal at the paralympics, 2012

Never say never... Everything is possible, if you have the will

Hans Dalal—Tiger, tiger, burning bright

Javed Abidi—Fighting for the rights of people with disability

Malathi Holla—Life is all about positivity

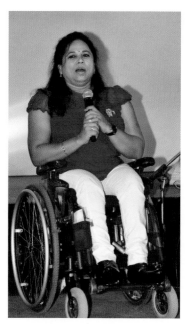

Champion of champions

Malvika Iyer—An inspiration for anyone who comes in contact with her

A flair for fashion. 'People with disability too want to wear stylish clothes', says Malvika

Mohammad Sharif performing at the Navjyoti Foundation's annual day

Outisde Navjyoti's campus. The foundation changed his life by introducing him to music

Ritwick and Roshan Rajan—Conquering hearts with their music

If music be the food of love

Siddharth GJ—A popular speaker

Telling his story to the world

Sundeep—Life is good if you can make people laugh

Life is a laugh...

Sunil Desai—Life is not always a smooth journey.
The key is living it without regrets

Caring for the community. Desai on one of his daily rounds
around his locality

Medicine Man Suresh Advani going through patient files at the hospital

Live every moment to the fullest...

in the discus throw and I was speechless with joy. That day I promised myself that training every single day would be a way of life for me. I repeated my success at the 1998 Asian Games, too, and built on my performance progressively, participating and snapping up gold and silver medals at the Open Championships in Belgium, Birmingham, and Manchester.

My medals from the Asian Games in Kuala Lumpur in 2006 remain some of my most cherished. With just under two months to train before I left for the event, I had little hope of winning anything. My competitors were formidable names in their countries and I felt my chances were zero and yet, at the end of the event, I had two silver medals in shot put and javelin. My heart filled with pride when I stood at the podium with the other winners. I was 48-years-old and I could feel a renewed confidence surge through my veins. Age and physical challenges are all in the mind. If you have determination, there is nothing that can stop you from getting what you want.

There have been many awards after that and great highs and lows in my career as a sportsperson. When I won the Arjuna award in 1979, it was a double victory for me since I had got a coveted recognition of my talent from the government of the country. What made it sweeter was the fact that I had got the award after a stubborn fight against a government rule that people with disability would not be eligible for this prestigious honour. I refused to let us be treated as second-class citizens when we actually work harder to bring laurels to the country. The government caved in finally and many disabled sportspersons have got the award since then.

When my name was announced in the list of Padma Shri

award winners in January 2001, it was like all the struggle and pain of my life had been more than worth it. I had brought honour to my country and to my family who had undergone a lot to give me a shot at life. On that memorable day, when President Shanker Dayal Sharma bestowed the award on me, my father broke down with joy. He was the one who gave me my strength and the spirit to never let my circumstances destroy me. His little daughter had grown up and brought glory to the family. I consider the Padma Shri my most valuable gift to my parents.

But if there have been great victories in my life, there have been situations that have crushed my spirit, too. I have learnt to take the good and the bad in my stride with equanimity. At the Birmingham Open Championships in 2005, I was elated when I won the gold medal in shot put and discus throw but that proved to be a short-lived happiness. Hours later, getting into the bus that would take the team back to our accommodation, I suffered a fall that left my right femur fractured. The nightmare worsened when doctors who attended to me said I was in need of surgery as soon as possible. With no one to attend to me in an alien country and with no way I could fund the surgery, I insisted that they bandage me up so that I could take the flight back to India the next day itself. It was one of the most painful journeys of my life but even in that situation, I noticed the kindness of a man who vacated his business class seat on that flight so that I could travel in some comfort. At the hospital, doctors performed emergency surgery on me, the thirty-second one in my life, inserting a plate to fix the broken bone. Unfortunately, just three months after that, I had to go in for another surgery because my body rejected the plate and was burning up with the pain of infection. For me, the nightmare is that I have gone from someone who was able to walk with the help of crutches to being completely wheelchair-bound after the accident and the two surgeries that followed.

But at each stage in life, I have used the pain in my life as a stepping stone to my next goal. Each of the surgeries have made me stronger, more determined, and resilient. I learnt early on that if you are strong, nothing can break down your self-belief or resolve. Everyone has disabilities. In some, it is physical and in others, it might be in the form of some emotional problem that is unseen. To my mind, the worst form of disability is the one which you bring upon yourself—an inferiority complex can be more crippling than a physical disability.

All of us face challenges in our life but what matters is how we overcome them. It is not enough to be woebegone and blame society for our problems. If you are the one that is affected by something, the onus is on you to either find a solution or work with the concerned people to find a resolution. For me, the struggle is constant. Even something as simple as going out for a cup of coffee is difficult because restaurant and café owners don't provide ramps that will allow people on wheelchairs to access the place. I've requested, begged, pleaded, cited the law, and used every kind of persuasion to make them understand that they must make their establishments more disabled-friendly, but to no avail. For me, the way ahead is simple—I keep up the pressure until they see reason!

I don't grumble about my life. I don't accept that something can be impossible to do or achieve, and I don't ever harbour the thought that I am inferior in some way because I don't have the use of my legs.

For many years, it was nagging away at the back of my mind that I was living a selfish life. I was revelling in my successes and was in a situation where, if I won a major medal, 50 percent of the credit would be mine, and the rest of it would be claimed by various others—by the state that I lived in and by the country. The media would say 'Malathi Holla from Karnataka, or Malathi Holla from India, and such other stuff.' But at night, when I lay on my bed, sleep would elude me because I would have this feeling that I was not giving back to the world that had given me so much. I have got so much from the people in the world of the disabled that I wanted to give back to them in some way. I am also aware that I am an ordinary mortal who might not be able to change the world but have it in my power to change myself.

A few years ago, I decided to spend some time each day in being of service to somebody. Even in the depths of our poverty, my father used to say that no matter how poor you are or how many physical problems you have, education is the one thing that will help you stand on your own feet in the society. Somewhere, the thought came into my mind that I should look after disabled children and give them an education so that they would not depend on anyone for their survival.

I was not sure I would be able to carry out this task alone but help was ready in the form of my friend, Krishna Reddy, who said he would support me from day one. Other friends joined quickly and before I knew it, the Mathru Foundation was up and running in 2005. Within the span of just eight years, I have become the proud mother of twenty children, all of who come from very poor rural homes where having a child with disability is not just considered a financial burden, but a curse.

With more mouths than they can feed and very little income, a disabled child is a prisoner confined to the hut because nobody has the time or the resources to educate him or look after his/her basic needs. And even if that child has a shining talent, that withers away from neglect. Over the last few years, we have been bringing such children to our centre, educating them, and raising them with good nutrition, discipline, confidence, and a sense of pride about themselves. They go to mainstream schools in the day and in the evening, they come back to the home we have built for them. It is a sort of hostel with basic facilities at the moment but eventually, I want to make it more comfortable for them and give them everything that kids of their age require.

Every step of the way is a challenge because it is not easy to fund the requirements of twenty children. My salary as a bank manager does not stretch enough to cover that and so my life is an endless round of visiting people with my begging bowl so people can donate. The government gives no aid because children with polio are expected to live with their family as per existing rules. So, I depend on the generosity of individuals who have a will to donate, such as the kind family who donated two pieces of land on which a larger Mathru home is coming up. Another friend reached out, connecting me with the architect firm which is helping us to build a disabled-friendly house. Along the way, I have developed a thick skin and great resilience. I don't want money for the kids but ask for things that will help them survive—bags of rice, dal, sugar, or vegetables. Once a year, we have to pay their school fees and luckily for me, people in the bank I work for and customers too, often help me with this. Since I am unmarried and have no other commitments, responsibilities, or financial worries, I am able to spend half of my salary to look after the children.

I believe that each of us is born on this earth with a reason. I think the reason I was born was so that I could give these children a better life. The memory of those children at the Chennai centre, abandoned by their families, remains in my mind till today and I think I am trying to create a better world for children, in whatever way I can.

While the rest of the world can only sympathize when they see a disabled child crawling on the ground, I can empathize because I know the physical and mental trauma that child is going through. I have lived that life and I understand their pain more than anyone else. I took up this cause so that I could raise them, show them the wonderful, colourful world they are born into. I want their lives to be an example for the rest of the world to follow. I want to tell the world, 'Look at us and live like us, and if you can't live like us, at least try to live like us.'

The journey of the last few years seems rewarding too when I see the impact Mathru has had on the lives of these kids. Many of the kids who come to us need focused medical attention and we have been able to fund multiple surgeries that have given a fair measure of independence to a few of them. Thanks to the training and education that we have been able to provide, a handful of them earn a livelihood for themselves that, even though not a great amount, has freed them from dependence on anyone. We now dream of taking the Mathru project further with plans for occupational training, an integrated school which will help mainstream my children while simultaneously help sensitize 'able' children to understand the less fortunate.

I think I have benefitted hugely in this journey because of my positivity. I have seen that there are lots of generous people who want to help but many are held back because they are not sure their resources will reach the people it was meant for. I have learnt that the world is like a mirror—if you look into it confidently, smilingly, enthusiastically, then it is a good world out there but if you look at it sulking and grumbly, it will look back at you in the same way.

Having come from where I did and having achieved things that even the able-bodied are not able to, has been a journey of discovery. I live for the moment and have learnt the virtue of acceptance. I never grumble, mope, or rant about it. If life gives me a beautiful experience or moment, I soak it up and revel in it because it makes me happy. I have eliminated sadness from my life. A few years ago, I was in love and engaged to be married, but suddenly one day that relationship ended because he did not want to marry a person with disability. I went through a very dark phase after that when I cursed my parents, the world, and the universe, questioning why I could not live like the rest of the world. I wanted a married life, I wanted to have my own children, and could not understand why the almighty had cruelly taken away all that from me. But as they say, behind every dark cloud there is a silver lining. The very next week, after the love of my life let me down, God gave me the opportunity to represent the country at the Asian Games. I had to leave Bengaluru and go to another city to train for the event. In retrospect, I know God had given me a beautiful opportunity to forget my heartbreak. I slogged for entire days on the training grounds, not to prove myself but to forget the pain of rejection and betrayal. I was a national-level champion athlete but I was consumed with my pain and kept wondering what mistakes I had committed for me to be punished so badly by God. But look at the miracle of life. Within months of a severe set-back in my life, I represented the country at a prestigious event and won a gold medal. That medal vindicated my struggle and the hard hours of gruelling training. But the more valuable part of the award, for me, was the fact that I was able to overcome the pain in my heart. Miraculously, that vanished and today I am able to look at my relationship with him in a positive light. He is now happily married and a father of two children.

My failed relationship is just one chapter in my life story. I have absolutely no regrets at all that it happened and failed to culminate in what I desired.

Now when I look back, I think there was a reason why that happened, too. If I had married him, I would have ended up within the four walls of our house, selfishly raising our own children. Today, I am mother to twenty children, even if I did not give birth to them. In the years to come, I want to become mother to many more children—at least a hundred. It might be a silly dream but it is my dream, and nobody can tell me to dream only sensible dreams.

I tell my kids that only a minute part of their body is disabled, but their determination and self-belief is not. I tell them, let your dreams and ambitions burn so bright inside you that they should not allow you to sleep at night. Motivation and inspiration lie within you. God has planted a seed in you and it is your job to nourish it with confidence, belief, punctuality, and discipline. When you do that you will start taking responsibility for your life instead of blaming others and life will become much easier.

Every now and then, when they have holidays at school, I take my children on outings where they can see and experience the world outside and learn from it. They have curious minds and they want to see the Parliament, the Taj Mahal, the big city life. It is not easy taking so many children with disabilities on a train trip but I use these journeys as another way of teaching them how to cope with unhygienic train toilets or about walking on their own on a moving train. I have a wonderful set of helpers who have been trained to handle my children on wheelchairs, getting them in and out of trains, and being sensitive to their needs. On every trip with them, I end up learning something more about life. It is our experiences that make us the people we are. Which is why, when given an opportunity, I believe each of us have to make the most of it.

I consider that being born as a person with a disability is God's gift to me. Had I been born like a normal person, like anybody else, I would have lived a very normal life, eating, drinking, sleeping, and living a life purely centred on my own needs. We live only once and to my mind, it is better to live like a servant rather than as a king!

I have come a long way from where I started my journey

but I am a very dissatisfied soul because there is so much more left for me to do. Every day that I live as a disabled person is a struggle but each second of that struggle also teaches me about life. The day I feel I'm content and I'm satisfied should be the last day of my life. My best is yet to come...

Malvika Iyer

The sketch visualizes Malvika as a young, blooming flower. The flower is born out of erasing the black patch with sharp silhouettes that indicates an explosion. The sketch encapsulates the entire experience of Malvika, showing the horrific explosion in the background and how she managed to carve out a happy, successful, and inspiring life for herself out of this situation that is depicted with a flower

The pencil around the corner with an eraser is a representative of her academic credentials.

Few things define the substance of human beings like their response to a challenging situation does. While most ordinary mortals like you and me would worry endlessly or collapse under the burden of the setback in our lives, there are others who take it in their stride and move ahead without letting it take centre stage in life.

It was late afternoon when I set out to meet Malvika Iyer at her house in Chennai and I was not sure if I had the address right as my cab driver weaved through the city's crowded lanes and by-lanes. 'Look for a blue house,' Malvika had told me and so I keep my eyes focused as the cabbie drove us through nondescript neighbourhoods teeming with hawkers selling their wares, till we reached the blue building where Malvika was waiting for me.

'Hi, I'm Malvika,' she said welcoming me with a firm handshake and laughter-filled eyes ablaze with life. We walked up the single flight of stairs that lead into the house she shared with her mother and it was only when I was halfway through my cup of hot tea that it dawned on me that Malvika had lost both her hands in an accident when she was a teenager. Nothing in her body language or the grip of the handshake had suggested to me that I was actually shaking hands with a prosthetic arm. Over the next few hours, I listened and watched in fascination as the radiant young woman recounted her journey of hope from being bed-ridden in hospital to someone who infuses life into everything and everyone with her *joie de vivre*.

When the organizers of the India Inclusion Summit (IIS) invited me to anchor the event in November 2013, introducing me as an inspiration to hundreds of thousands of differently-abled people in our country, I felt immensely proud of myself. Not because I think I am superior to others but because by being on that platform, I was able to demonstrate to the world that being differently-abled is not a curse or a burden for those in that situation. I celebrate each day of my life. There is so much that I look forward to everyday, I have so much in my life to be grateful for, so much I can do to improve the lives of those like me in this country. To me, 'disability' is a perception in the minds of other people. My reality is different from the reality of the majority in this country, but that is the only difference. I am made from the same stuff as everybody else is. As a child roaming around the residential colony in Bikaner in Rajasthan, where I lived with my parents and elder sister, I had not a care in the world. I climbed trees, played on the street with the neighbourhood boys, took swimming and skating lessons, and was not the least interested in studies. All that changed the day I picked up and got home with a grenade that I found in the neighbourhood, after the local ammunition factory had caught fire and scattered small ammo all around. We had thought the grenade was diffused and left it in our garage where it lay dangerously silent till the day it exploded, changing my life in a way nobody could have imagined.

I still remember that day vividly. I wandered into the garage and picked up the grenade, placing it on my knee as I sat down. In that instant, the grenade exploded and my body was ablaze with pain. My father and a friend who heard the explosion rushed in and when they saw me in that condition, they put me in a jeep and headed to the nearest government hospital. That is when I noticed that my left leg was dangling by a small piece of skin. 'Please hold my leg. It is falling off', I remember telling them.

My parents told me that the first night in hospital the doctors were not sure I would survive since I had lost 80 percent of the blood in my body but somehow, I managed to hang on to my life. The next morning, however, the doctors told my parents that my left leg would have to be amputated since it was impossible to contain the infection that had spread through it. Shattered, my parents refused to heed their suggestion and, at their own risk, shifted me to a bigger hospital in Jaipur where the doctors managed to save my legs and slowly pieced them back over the next few days. Lying on the hospital bed the reality dawned on me that I had lost both my arms from below the elbows and that I would probably never use both my legs again. My legs had suffered multiple fractures, my right leg was paralysed, pieces of shrapnel were embedded deep inside them, and in some places the bones were crushed into tiny pieces, leaving my legs severely disfigured.

It took a long time—well, two years is a long time for a teenager to be bed-ridden—and multiple surgeries before I was finally able to hope for some normalcy in life. After the initial few months in Jaipur, when the doctors could not do anything more to help me, my mom decided to shift me to Chennai where her side of the family lived. Thankfully for me, doctors at the Bone and Joint Clinic in the city were able to complete the process that started in Jaipur. After six months in hospital and one and a half years bed-ridden at home, the doctors told me in December 2003 that I could start walking a bit with the help of crutches. For me, it was the start of my life all over again.

Back home in Bikaner, my friends were preparing for their exams and suddenly, I too felt the need to write my 10th grade exams but there was no way that I could do it since I had been away from school since 8th grade. It was here that my mother stepped in, continuously doing the rounds of schools, but no one wanted to take in a girl so late in the academic year, especially one who could not even walk and had no hands. A cousin of mine then directed me to a coaching class which prepared students to give their 10th grade exams privately and after much pleading, I eventually convinced the owner of the class to allow me to give it a shot. When I walked into that coaching class that day, it was the first time that I was stepping out in over a year and a half, and it was the strangest feeling to see real people my age around me. It was also awkward because back then, I was this frumpily dressed girl with wild hair (they cut off my flowing locks because it was impossible to manage it while I was bed-ridden) and no hands, and I had very little communication skills left after so much time spent by myself.

It was a taxing time for an adolescent. My mother understood the situation instantly and soon, we were feverishly searching for artificial hands till one day, we found a pair of myoelectric hands that were perfect for me. Outfitted in my new clothes and a brand new pair of arms, I was back to being my old, cheerful self. My self-confidence got a major boost when the exam results came in a couple of months later and I discovered, to my utter disbelief, that I had score 97 percent marks with cent percent marks in both Math and Science. I believe that was the turning point of my life. I had never done so well in academics before and I was more shocked than happy that this had happened. The owner of the coaching class was so overjoyed, he informed the local newspapers about my achievement and before I knew it, I was a celebrity—the brave girl without arms who had conquered her circumstances to achieve something.

I remember enjoying the limelight but through all of it, I was always a little embarrassed when they wanted me to display the stumps of my arms. *How is that important*, I wondered but today, I think it was alright because it is that accident and my refusal to give up on myself that had given me a new life. It was not easy coming out of the phase when I was constantly in and out of hospitals. Relatives, friends, and strangers would pity me and stare, and give unwanted advice. 'She is a girl and she is now disabled. You will never manage to get her married,' they would tell my parents and I would shrink in horror from listening to their insensitive comments. Somehow, my parents and family kept me protected and safe in that traumatic phase of my life.

Soon after I got my prosthetic arms, I started grooming myself and making friends. Since I had always been a talkative person, making friends was never a difficult thing for me but sometimes I would feel a bit inferior because of my arms. I had never met or seen anyone with a disability, especially someone with no arms, and the fact that I was now a girl in that situation arms bothered me sometimes. Thankfully, those were temporary phases and I sailed through my 12th grade exams, studying Commerce and Economics without being bogged down by my thoughts.

When it was time for me to sign up for college, I told my parents I wanted to graduate with a degree in Economics from St Stephen's College in Delhi. My parents were more than willing to let me go there and when I asked my mom, she willingly stayed with me while I studied. That is how my mother is. The day my accident happened, she just gave up the rest of her life—her husband, my sister, everybody. From that day until today she has been like a friend and a trusted roommate who is constantly by my side. I'm lucky to have the boundless love of my family and friends who never looked at me differently because suddenly, I had no arms and disfigured legs to boot!

The five years I spent in Delhi till I completed my post-graduation from the Delhi School of Social Work was a learning experience. The fieldwork curriculum brought me in touch with the ground realities of our country and the society around me. My very first fieldwork experience was at the Centre for Child and Adolescent Well Being, Delhi, where I taught children with learning disability and kids who came under the Autistic Spectrum Disorder (ASD). By the time I was halfway through the course, I fell in love with the subject and the fieldwork projects which brought me in touch with different kinds of people, each with their own set of problems. Slowly, I became aware of how skewed our society is against people with various types of disability.

At one of the first places where I went for a fieldwork job, I realized the very first day that the lady in charge was hesitant to hire me because I was disabled. I heard her telling somebody that she wanted to hire another person because she did not think I would be able to do much. But by the next day, she had changed her mind when she realized how much work I had done. She herself came up to me and said she never imagined I would be able to contribute to the extent I had done.

People have a lot of misconceptions about people with disabilities but they don't know that we are capable of exactly the same things that normally-abled people are. All we need is to be given a chance to use our skill and talent.

Back in Chennai, I signed up for my MPhil and used my own experiences to do research on the quality of life of people with orthopaedic disability. The research work I did for my MPhil project, my visits to various rehabilitation centres, and my meetings with several people with disabilities helped me discover a lot of myself. I was able to dispel the myth that people with disability are either unhappy, frustrated, or depressed. Far from it. While normally-abled people have a lot to complain about their lives, I found people with disability to generally be people very much at peace with who they are and the realities in their life. Till today, I am amazed at the energy and the zest for life that the disabled have. I, too, became happier when I learnt to accept myself the way I was. When I got the Rolling Cup for the best research thesis of that year, I felt vindicated and happy that I was able to put across the point of the view of the disabled to the rest of the population.

If I were to identify the one thing that has changed the course of my life and prevented it from being one of misery, that factor would have to be 'inclusion'. I remember one Diwali season when my mother and I were at home in Bikaner immediately after my accident. I was in bed and in great pain when a neighbour came home to invite us for a party. My mum declined because she was not in the right frame of mind to socialize. A few days later we realized there was another party in the neighbourhood and this time we were not invited. It was not a nice feeling because we had always been part of every social event in our gated community. My mother walked over to the neighbour and said she was wondering why we were not invited to the Diwali bash. The neighbour had this to say to us: 'The last time we came over with an invitation you were in a very angry mood so we thought that since your family has been in a tragedy, maybe you don't want to be a part of any kind of happiness anymore.' That is when it struck my mom and me that it is our own attitude that decides how people will react to us. People are going to like you, but if you try to shut yourself out from life, nobody's going to ever like you. After that day, we never said no to anything.

The effect of inclusion has been life-changing for me. My parents could have given up on me and kept me home without much bothering about giving me education or any other skills. Instead, I was blessed to have parents who gave me access to different kinds of experiences, a great education, and a very normal childhood. Through my motivational talks in schools and other platforms, including TEDx, I have been able to spread the word about inclusion and its impact on the disabled. When she heard about the NGO Ability Foundation's short film contest on 'Celebrating Inclusion', my mother decided to make a short, one-minute film on my life, recording everything from the time I wake up, to doing my chores before going to college or work using public transport and then heading out to meet my friends. I thought it was a ridiculous idea but she stuck to her guns and was vindicated when the film, *The Phoenix*, was shortlisted for that year's award.

Enthused by the fact that my work is striking a chord in the minds of people, I have now signed up for a PhD, through which, I will examine the issue of inclusion and exactly how 'included'the disabled in this country feel. I will also try and figure out the attitude of normally-abled people towards those with disability.

Over the years, I have been invited to a lot of schools and colleges as a motivational speaker to talk about my life. Many people find my journey inspiring; I, myself, think each of us need some inspiration in our lives. I was once at a hospital when a girl seated near me introduced herself and said she had seen me on television the week before. I was astonished when she started crying and told me that she was in the middle of a stand-off with her family and was frustrated because she was dependent on them. Then she firmly wiped her eyes clean and said that she no longer felt afraid. 'If you have lost both your hands and have achieved so much despite that, why should I feel scared or vulnerable? I am able-bodied and will make my own life,' she said.

I often tell people that life is so short that it is a crime not to maximize that time. Before the accident, I was a trained Kathak dancer and missed it terribly in the years that I was incapacitated. Today, I've gone back to dancing, the only difference being that I now do western forms of dancing that do not require extensive use of arms like they do in Kathak. I can't dance with as much ease as before but I am happy to be dancing because I think it is in my blood.

Since I was bedridden for such a long time, I was able to introspect and think about my life and in that process, I discovered a liking for writing poetry. This just goes to show that everything in our life can be converted into an opportunity. You just have to inculcate the right attitude. My mother never raised me differently from my elder sister and never gave me the luxury of pity. With her stern attitude, she made sure I was independent and self-reliant, and I am glad she did that because pity is a dangerous thing. It makes you crave it and makes you dependent on someone to do your stuff for you.

It is my self-reliant and independent stance that also brought me close to the man who I will marry in a couple of years. I met him on a social networking site and our friendship carried on for a long time before we met face to face and found that we wanted to be together forever. When I announced that I had a boyfriend who I wanted to marry, the first question almost everyone asked me was if he was also disabled like me. It took me a long time to convince them it is perfectly possible for a differently-abled person to fall in love and marry somebody who is normally-abled and vice versa. I am blessed to have met a man whose family took to me instantly.

In the years to come, I want to explore a career in counselling because I think my own experiences and the field work stints have made me a more sensitive person. My stint with the Schizophrenia Research Foundation (SCARF) left a deep impression on me because I realized how disadvantaged patients suffering from the condition are. At some point I would love to work in that space, too.

Right now, I am involved in a project that is, literally, 'right up my sleeve'. For years, I have struggled to find readymade clothes in store that fit my prosthetic arm, but to no avail. People who use prosthetic arms or legs know that the sockets are bulky and need roomier sleeves to fit properly. At some point, I gave up, and mom and I started designing and tailoring my own clothes so that I could feel elegant with my prosthetic arm. I have always had an interest in fashion and I am now helping in a project started by the National Institute of Fashion Technology and Ability Foundation to design clothes for the disabled. I am doubling as their model and also a consultant who is helping them understand that it is not just about designing practical clothes—those with disability want to wear clothes that make them look good, too!

At every step along the way, my life has been about pushing myself to my limits and each time, I have discovered new strengths and talents within me. My biggest mission when I started walking after my accident was to climb the stairs up to my house. At one time, it was as formidable a task as climbing a mountain but today, I am able to run up the whole staircase.

The key is to stay inspired and motivated. A few months ago, I went on a 3 km trek in Ooty and even though my legs hurt a lot and kept me in bed for an entire day afterwards, I enjoyed the experience.

Though I have an electronic hand, it can't do everything for me. I use it to write, when I go out in public, and for cosmetic purpose. Everything else I do with my real hands. Even if they are just stubs, I can type very easily with them. In fact, I have typed my entire MPhil thesis with them.

Because of my physical disability, I always felt the need to compensate by being well-groomed and looking good. Psychologically, it made me feel stronger when I was well turned out and this led to an interest in makeup and cosmetics. Today, I am able to use myoelectric arm to do the delicate job of applying kajal, mascara, and eye shadow. I need help with my bindi though, and my mom does that for me.

Many a time people ask me what inspires me. I am inspired by people who treat me just the same way they treat normally-abled people. I want all of us to understand that the moment you treat us differently, it is shutting us out of your life completely. The differently-abled don't need sympathy; they just need to be in a space where they are not judged by others or measured by societal perceptions of who they are and what they are capable of.

My own motto about life is very simple. Fight and you will survive, surrender and you will be wiped out.

Mohammad Sharif

Mohammad Sharif has his left hand showing a thumb up gesture characteristic of his positive attitude, readiness for challenges, and a reflection of his success. His gesture is also enveloped with a musical note to indicate that music is his passion and identity. The musical note has a harmonium embedded within and has just one arm (subtle representation of his condition). Hence, the sketch is well-rounded, which brings all the elements of the story together.

I met Mohammad Sharif on a sweltering summer afternoon when there was not even a whisper of a breeze to cool the parched earth. I had spent the entire first part of the day flying to Delhi and taking a seemingly endless cab drive to get to the tiny village outside Gurgaon where I was to meet my friend Ferose, who had set up a lovely little music school dedicated to his son with Navjyoti, an NGO run by retired IPS officer Kiran Bedi, a woman I grew up admiring. But all the fatigue of my mind and body disappeared just as soon as a group of village youngsters started singing a soul-stirring Sufi song, ably led by their smiling teacher, Mohammad Sharif, who played the harmonium.

It was only when the group finished the song and folded their hands to acknowledge the thundering applause from the audience that I noticed something: Mohammad Sharif had played the harmonium with his left hand and right leg! He does not have a right arm at all!

My early life was spent in Nanpara, a forgotten little village in the heart of Uttar Pradesh where I lived with my family of five siblings and my parents. If there is one thing that I remember of those early years, it is the stark poverty that stared us in the face every single day. My parents were illiterate and slaved endlessly for various landowners, whose fields they worked in so that they could feed their six children. And because they were away for most of the day, my siblings and I spent the days with our grandparents who lived in the neighbourhood. Looking back, I think that the poverty and the constant shortage of even the most basic things never made a difference in our lives. We were too young to notice that we did not have anything much in life other than the rationed-out portions of two meals a day. But even so, I spent my days happily running around in the fields with my friends. Studies were only a small part of our existence and we went to school only because we had to.

And then one day, all of that changed. Since my grandparents were too old to go to the market or get their everyday chores done, we children helped them by running errands. On that particular day, it was my turn to take the wheat to the flour mill so that my nani could make rotis for our dinner. My friend and I handed over our wheat bags to the flour mill owner and hung around watching the wheat being crushed by the giant electric mortar, the speedy conveyor belt that made the entire thing work, and how the finely ground flour emerged magically from the gaping jaws at the other end of the machine. Even after all these years, I am still not able to fathom how exactly I managed to get myself entangled in that machine. One moment, we were standing by its side and the next, I felt myself being dragged by my right hand and before I knew what was happening, my hand had got entangled in the crushing machine and it had managed to wrench it off my shoulder socket! I remember my shocked child's eyes watching my hand being swallowed up by the machine and thrown out at the other end, all crushed. I remember the commotion around me as people shouted and my friend's attempt to save me, but nothing after that. When I woke up, I was lying on a hospital bed and my parents were by my side, my mother sobbing her heart out. I weaved in and out of consciousness for a few days but woke up one morning, fully conscious. My father told me that the sleeve of my *kurta* had got entangled in the machine that pulled me in. What he said after that was even more shocking: my friend who tried to save me had also got his hand entangled in the machine, in a bid to save me. Thankfully, he had managed to escape with just a fractured arm, but I, on the other hand, lost my arm in the accident.

My class teacher was also at my bedside when I regained consciousness. He was a kind man who always had good things to say to his students. That day, at the hospital, he said something that set the tone for the rest of my life: 'All kinds of things happen to us. This is what God has destined for you but that does not mean you have lost out on the rest of your life.

You have to overcome this setback and move on. I will help you start the rest of your life.' I did not understand the significance of the message the simple village school teacher was giving me but somehow, I think, he guessed that lying on that hospital bed I had thought that I would not have any fun in life because I had lost my right hand. I thought I would not be able to go to school or play *gilli danda* with my friends or ever learn to play a musical instrument. I belong to a community that has traditionally made and sold *dholaks*, and even though our poverty prevented us from spending time on that profession, I had a strong urge in me to play it, and I wanted to learn it from my father. *That would never be possible*, I had thought, when I woke up in the hospital bed and realized I had only one hand left.

But miraculously, the kind school teacher's words worked their magic on me when he turned up the very next day and started teaching me to hold a pencil and write with my left hand. It was a laborious and frustrating experience but he never lost his patience or gave up on me. Back home from the hospital, I practiced hard to write legibly and my efforts soon bore fruit when I was able to write effortlessly with my left hand and could go back to school.

Two years after my accident, however, my parents decided to leave our village and head to the big city, in search of a better future for us. We children were puzzled by our parent's decision because they grew up in that village, but one day *abba* said that I would have very little future in a village, given that I was a disabled person now. I did not know it when we boarded the train to Delhi, but it was a journey that would set the course of the rest of my life.

Delhi was not at all like what we had imagined. We had thought the streets would be paved with magnificent houses, but the reality was different. We landed under the shadows of the imposing Lal Quila, in Yamuna Pushta, a miserable community of shanties in those days. All around us were people even poorer than us and there was dirt and filth everywhere. But what shocked us were the gangs of young boys and men who roamed around the shanty, engaging in criminal activities and openly flouting the laws. They feared no one, teased women, robbed people, and lived in a world where only they ruled. When I look back today, I thank our stars that none of us ended up joining one of the gangs. Instead, we children kept to ourselves, went to the Lal Quila school and spent our evenings doing our lessons. My father picked up the threads of his old family profession—making and selling *dholaks*—and joined a group of others engaged in the same activity in our settlement. Finally, I was able to get a glimpse of the traditional skill that our family had.

Right from my childhood, I remember being fascinated by singing, and I would always roam around in my free time with a small radio stuck to one ear. At home, the radio was always playing and entertaining us with old filmy music or other forms of music. I was so fond of singing that I would harass my father into listening to my songs whenever he was home. I never imagined that one day my destiny would lead me into a career in music.

In 1987, when I was in the 7th grade at school, IPS officer Kiran Bedi came to our settlement and opened a branch of her NGO, Navjyoti . She was already a reputed police officer who had made a name for herself in rehabilitating criminals and for offering women and children ways to develop and improve their lives. Our settlement, full of migrant labour from all parts of the country who took to crime due to unemployment, was a place that urgently needed her attention. Then, miraculously for me, I got an opportunity through their social workers to go and teach the kids at Navjyoti's school. I was awed at the prospect but enjoyed being in the company of children who seemed to like me a lot. In addition to teaching them alphabets and activities, I taught them to act which, too, was my passion, and soon, we were all having a great time. It is said that God looks after those who believe in him. The team at Navjyoti realized my passion for acting and sent me to a neighbourhood acting school to further develop my talent. It was a joyful moment for me when I returned after completing my acting course and was promptly employed as a drama teacher to the kids at Navjyoti, and I took up the challenge, directing them in street plays and impromptu performances.

In 1990, Navjyoti appointed its first music teacher at our settlement and that was the beginning of another chapter of my life. Since I was now a teacher at the school, I could not find the time to attend his music class but after school I would go and listen to him and sometimes request him to hear me sing. Arjun Kumarji was a generous teacher and a large-hearted man. He was quick to catch my passion for music and one day, he said that I should learn to play the harmonium if I was serious about music. I thought he was making fun of me but he said he would teach me to play the instrument with my right leg as a substitute for my right arm. His belief in me filled me with hope and soon we got busy with the task. It was challenging, frightening, and very painful. During the initial days, my toes developed blisters that were very painful, then came the calluses, and on some days, walking was impossible because my foot hurt a lot, but I stuck to my decision and continued to play the instrument.

Soon I had learnt the *sargam*, *alankar*, and *raag* from my music teacher and I was overjoyed when he said one day that he had filled out a form for me to learn music at the Allahabad Prayag Sangeet Samiti. It was possibly the most joyous day of my life when I got admission there. I had always dreamt of being a singer and a musician, and the years I spent at the institute made me the person I aspired to be. When I left the institute at the age of 22, I had a Masters in Music and a life full of promise.

Almost as soon as I returned from Allahabad, I was appointed by Kiran Bedi as a music teacher at Navjyoti and that was the beginning of the next chapter of my life. Over the last fifteen years, I like to think that I have not just taught music to the poor children who come to Navjyoti, but in my own way, I have brought some joy into the lives of these children who live each day in the most daunting conditions. Music ,therefore, becomes an escape for them and also a future source of livelihood. Just as I sing at weddings, cultural programmes, and *qawwali* sessions, these children, too, will find their own platforms and their own students to whom they can pass on their skill.

Over the last few years at Navjyoti, I have been teaching 3–4 batches, each comprising of thirty underprivileged kids every day, and I am grateful that I have been given the task of bringing some meaning into their lives. When I hear them humming a song or playing a musical instrument, I feel the same pride that I do when I see my own children taking joy in music. In the years I have been with Navjyoti, I must have taught at least a thousand children. Though I have lost count now, but each kid I teach gives me fresh joy. When we spot especially talented children at the Navjoyti centre, we send them to other music schools, too, so that their skills are further honed. Saddam, a young boy of 8–9 years started learning music from me at Navjyoti centre at the Bawana Resettlement Colony situated in the north west part of Delhi and is now a proficient harmonium player and *ghazal* singer at the age of 16. When I see him perform at talent shows and competitions, I feel a great sense of pride.

My father taught me to play the *dholak* with one hand and I knew then, that everything is possible if we work hard towards making it possible. Even today, when I tell people that I am a musician and can play the harmonium and the *dholak*, they find it hard to believe till they see me perform. But I never let their disbelief or condescension affect me.

Some days, when I pass through the by-lanes of the community where I live, my heart swells with joy when little kids who learn music from me point out to me and greet me, giggling and singing *sa re ga ma!*

From where my family came, and given our abject poverty, there would have been no future for us. My father worked very hard to put his kids through school and believed in their dreams. My own children are all educated and share my love for music. One of my sons has been fortunate enough to be sponsored by Navjyoti to become a trained classical dancer, and is now learning western dance forms. So each day, I thank God for his kindness. If not for him and for my father's insistence on educating his kids and giving wings to their dreams, I probably would have ended up as a beggar people threw alms at out of pity for my disability. Instead, I live a life of dignity as a teacher and a musician who is respected for his art. What more could I have asked for in life?

Ritwick

and

Roshan Rajan

The narrative has not one character, but a unit of three characters, and their interlocking relationships forms the essence of the story. The sketch brings about amma in the centre who is really like the spine or the backbone of the story, holding all things together. The heart shape could be seen as her motherly selfless love and the same shape is also used to bring about her two boys (quite a literal overlap) and the trio embracing each other, consolidating and merging into one single entity—an epitome of love in its pure iconic form.

In a modest house on the outskirts of Bengaluru, surrounded by trees and flowering shrubs, and by their love for each other, lives a family whose story is incredible in many ways. A young woman gave birth to a blind child and devoted herself to him. Years later, when she felt that her child was lonely, she decided to have another child. Unfortunately, her second son, too, was born blind. Only, this time it was worse—her second born was not just blind but had multiple disabilities as well. A fighter, the woman decided to raise her children in a way that would give them fulfilling lives. I visited their home one evening expecting to just talk to her sons but got to know a family whose commitment to each other left me fascinated and humbled. The two young people I was to interview were blind but when I met them, I knew that they never realized they were blind because they saw life in all its glory through the eyes of their mother. They have travelled to various corners of the world, have captivated diverse audiences, and have a fan base all over the country. They might never have seen the sky but for their aspirations the sky is the limit.

❧

Roshan Rajan

When my parents were really young, I was born to them, blind. They took me to different doctors but returned disappointed because the doctors said there was nothing they could do to save the situation. My mother, a working woman, decided that she would bring me up to the best of her abilities and that meant not treating me any different from the way she would have treated a normally-abled child.

I was not an easy child to bring up because she tells me that I would stay up crying all night, and so they learnt to keep me entertained by playing the tape recorder besides me at night. By the time I was 2–3 years of age, I was familiar with all types of songs and music. She says that I first picked up a sense of rhythm from the pitter-patter of water falling from the tap in the bathroom while she bathed me or washed clothes. That sense of rhythm and my early exposure to music led to a lifelong fascination for it. Today, music is a large part of life for both me and my brother Ritvik, who is ten years younger to me and is blind, too. In fact, I would say that since he is autistic and does not talk much, music is life itself for him.

Since none of the schools in our locality would admit a blind student, my mother, who had no idea what to do with her son, took me to a neighbourhood singing class where a lady taught Carnatic music. My first music teacher was a kind soul who allowed me to attend her classes a couple of times a week and thus, I ended up learning music when my cousins, the same age as me, were learning alphabets! Though I have no memory of this, my mother tells me that I took to music easily and was so good at it that once, when the teacher had to go out of class for a little while, I stepped in and took over, leading the class in reciting some *shlokas*.

When I was 4 years old, I started learning the musical instrument *Mridangam* and got my first chance to perform in public on *Akashvani*. A senior artist who was supposed to perform on *Akashvani* could not attend the event and so, my *bhajan* teacher recommended my name for that slot. I have faint memories of singing while *mamma* stood holding the *mridangam* for me because I was too tiny to hold it myself! Little did I know that the first performance would lead me to a career with *Akashvani* where I am a regular artist today and a voice that many are familiar with.

Those first years in the *bhajan* class were followed by years of training in Carnatic music, *mridangam*, keyboard, and violin. Because of our father's transferable job, we kept travelling to different towns such as Hyderabad and Mysore, and in 1998, when I was about 17–18 years old, the family shifted to the town of Dharwad. There were no Carnatic music teachers in that place, and so, with much worry, I had to switch to learning Hindustani music. That was initially difficult but I soon picked up the nuances of Hindustani music too because by nature I am musically inclined. I learnt Hindustani music for seven years before my father was transferred back to Bengaluru.

I was 10 years old when Ritvik, my brother, was born. He too, was born blind, but as a couple of years went by, my parents realized that he had other problems as well—he did not speak at all and had very poor motor movements, and the doctors soon told them he could be autistic. Because he was totally dependent on them even for everyday stuff such as eating, they could not bear to send him to the neighbourhood special school because that happened to be a residential facility and he would have never been able to cope on his own.

My own childhood was as normal as I can imagine. I started attending a mainstream school while in Upper KG, and *mamma* says I was notorious because I used to pick fights with other kids, and she was always trying to get me out of trouble. *Mamma* learnt braille when I was still a toddler and tutored me at home much before I joined the mainstream school where with the help of a resource teacher I kept pace with the class. In fact, *mamma* made sure that I was way ahead of the class in lessons—if the teacher was teaching the class their lesson number two, she would make sure I was already on lesson eight!

For a long time I never realized what it meant to be blind. *Mamma* would take me with her everywhere—to the bank, the post office, and to the grocery shop where I was made to touch and feel everything that we bought for the house. She even took me saree shopping and would describe the colour of the saree that she was buying and the patterns and prints on it. Much later, when I was about 10–11 years of age, I would go with the domestic help and buy bangles, earrings, and *bindis* for *mamma* to match the colour of her favourite sarees.

During my primary school days, a few boys in class started teasing and taunting me, calling me blind. 'What is blind?' I remember asking my mother one day, and she pulled me to her gently and asked me why I was asking that question. I told her about the bullying at school, the taunts and the jibes, and she asked me, 'What do you feel and see with?' I said, 'I feel with my fingers'. She asked, 'How many eyes do we have?' And I said, 'two eyes,' and she said to me then, 'If you are seeing with ten fingers and others are seeing with just two eyes, which is better?' In many ways, that discussion with *Mamma* was the turning point in my life. She told me that day, "You are better off than them because you can see with ten fingers and also with my eyes, while they can see with just two eyes, so there's no question of blindness at all. Everybody is blind in their own way.'

When I went to school the next day, I had with me a sheet of paper in which she had written something in braille. She asked me to call my tormentors and challenge them to read out what was written on the braille sheet. And when they failed to do that, I said to them, 'This is my language and since you are not able to read it, you are blind, too.' The teasing at school did not stop completely but since the conversation with my mother, the bullying did not matter so much. In fact, I think it made me stronger.

By this time, I started finding academics uninteresting, and just when I thought I could give it up after my pre-university course, my mother stepped in, insisting that I finish my graduation, and when I finished that, she insisted I do my MA in English, which, too, I did, albeit reluctantly.

I was passionate about music by then and was ready to try my luck with the film industry in Bengaluru, which is the land of opportunity. But Bengaluru's booming Information Technology sector enchanted me with its promise of a livelihood that would allow me to stand on my own feet. My enthusiasm soon turned into depression when companies rejected me because they did not believe a blind person could operate a computer. And this despite the fact that I had passed a computer training course conducted by the National Association for the Blind with distinction. I told them that with the talking software—JAWS—I could do almost everything a sighted person could do, but to no avail. Eventually I ended up working for four years at a BPO in the city because I was simply not confident of taking up a teaching job, like my mother wanted me to. By now, Ritvik was also heavily into music, and between the two of us, we made a great pair. But a career in the film industry continued to elude us because the Karnataka film industry is heavily influenced by Bollywood singers and would much rather have an artist from there sing for their film, than local talent. It used to bother me when I would be called to record a song for a movie but when the film would release, I would realize that my voice had been replaced with somebody else's.

At school, especially in Mysore, where we lived for some time, I remember my teachers used to call me to perform in different classes, sometimes even to diffuse tension during difficult times. *Mamma* also used to make me take part in singing competitions where I often got the first prize, but I was nowhere near professional at that point.

Our first break came in April 2004 when the Bengaluru Art Lovers Association (BALA) approached us to perform at one of their functions. Somebody from the organization had heard us sing at a family wedding and remembered our voice enough to want us to perform for them. It was a great evening where we presented a medley of songs that included classical, *ghazals*, *qawwali*, and film songs to the audience. Between us, Ritvik and I sing in seven Indian languages, even though Ritvik does not speak in any language other than English. But he is great at picking up songs and rendering them perfectly! For the better part of his life, he has had a peculiar habit of responding to people by singing out situation-appropriate snatches from songs! It is a shared joke in the family but visitors are often flummoxed by it because they can't figure out how somebody who is unable to speak fluently is able to sing effortlessly.

Before we knew it, we were performing at dozens of events with just word-of-mouth publicity. Organizations such as the Lions and Rotary Clubs supported us and gave us a platform, as did music lovers in Bengaluru, who loved the variety in our repertoire. Word of our performance got a television channel, NDTV, interested enough to do a documentary on us which was followed, almost immediately, by a Bengaluru-based organization bestowing their Young Achievers award on us in 2005.

In 2007, Ritvik got the opportunity to participate in Asianet channel's Idea Star Singer program and that made him a very popular singer, noticed and admired wherever he went. His presence there further enhanced our standing in the public space, and demand for our performance increased. The next year we both appeared on their Kannada channel's Confident Singer show, and it was a learning and fun experience but we eventually, gave up because travelling repeatedly for the shoot was a logistics nightmare for *mamma*. In the last 14–15 years, we have performed on at least a thousand different platforms and each time, we come away thankful for the chances that life has given us. Sometime in 2008, we joined visually impaired activist George Abraham's band, Magic Touch, and the next year, I got an opportunity through this platform to sing at the royal palace of Jordan, with the king himself in the audience. Later, both he and the queen met me and appreciated our uniqueness. That trip abroad and the opportunity to sing with reputed artists including Vasundhara Das, is a cherished memory as is the time singer Adnan Sami encouraged me as I was slowly building my career.

December 2011 was the beginning of an altogether new journey when we started our own music school. Since we were both blind, it was necessary for our parents to plan carefully for our future so that we would not suffer after they had passed away. I already had a job of my own but Ritvik was dependent to a fairly high degree, so she said it would be wise to figure out a way in which we would have an assured livelihood for ourselves.

Since our parents were already building a house for us in Bengaluru they decided to build one storey that would be dedicated to a music school that we could start. Today, the pride that we experience when parents come with their little kids to learn music from us, in the big music room that they built for us atop our house, is indescribable. It is our dream to someday build a recording studio of our own so that we can pursue our passion for music even further. It is a long haul because it is an expensive dream, and we don't make enough money for such expensive pursuits, but our parents save all the money that we earn and so I am confident that we will get our own recording studio. *Mamma* always tells me that it is important to keep trying. If you run into a wall or a barrier, knock it down and move ahead—she says—and I know that is what she did when she had to raise us as a young working mother.

From the way she raised us, I know that persistence and faith are important if one has to get towards a goal. When doctors told her that in addition to being blind, Ritvik also has multiple disabilities, she did not give up. Instead, she focused her entire energy to teach him braille—his motor movement meant that it took her eighteen months to just teach him to hold the stylus to be used for the braille—and then she worked with him till he started piecing words and sentences together at the age of 9. Even today, most of his communication is through the medium of music but he is able to communicate fluently. When he became the youngest earning member of our family at the age of 9, singing in a female voice at various events, it was a vindication of her belief in him and in the tenacity of the human spirit.

One of the most important lessons we learnt from our parents is about the power of self-belief. It was this belief that led me to set up the music club at the BPO where I worked. I noticed that there were lots of employees there who were musically talented but were stressed out and bored in their jobs. I thought I knew how to take the monotony out of their lives and began teaching them voice modulation. Since I am a good teacher, they grasped things quickly and eventually, we formed our own band, performing at corporate shows and other platforms. It was a very happy phase of my life because I felt I had created something on my own. That success led us to cutting an album of our own, with thirteen songs. 24/7, the BPO we worked at, funded the album but due to circumstances beyond our control, that album could not be released. Nevertheless, putting it together was a priceless experience and my confidence grew leaps and bounds.

People ask me sometimes about Ritvik's unique relationship with music. To me, his is a different kind of music altogether and a journey that is brave and fearless. From a blind, savant child to a musical prodigy who has let nothing stop him from conquering a variety of obstacles to make music of his own, his is an inspirational journey that each of us can learn from. When *mamma* realized that he could not speak fluently but had a keen ear for music, she used her wisdom to get him to learn the keyboard, *tabla*, and to pass any number of exams with splendid grades. Last year he completed his Hindustanti Visharad from the Gandharva Mahavidyalaya, Miraj, becoming the highest scorer amongst the visually impaired candidates in India who appeared for the exam.

But that is only one part of the story. The other part, that continues to fascinate everyone is the part where she and he worked slowly together to get past his problem with motor movements till he had a great typing speed. Determined that her son pass 10th grade exams, *mamma* enrolled him in the

National Open School. It was a huge challenge because it is difficult for anyone to explain any concepts to him but she decided to make it happen by recording his notes, reading out each line and sentence thrice so that he was able to grasp it. For spellings, she had another cassette that she kept playing to him. Their favourite thing to do while they travelled in a rickshaw to his music class was to play vocabulary games. Ritvik cleared his secondary examination from NIOS with distinction. Today, his spellings and vocabulary are very good and he is able to speak in a limited manner. But his aspirations are without limits. He tells the world that he wants to become a singer just like Justin Beiber.

Ritvik's music class is also a unique collaboration with *mamma*—she makes sure his students are disciplined and pay attention while he sings for them. She gives the instructions for them to follow his singing. It is our family's joy that Ritvik is today a music teacher who is in great demand in our locality, and is even teaching a few autistic students . The Delhi Public School, Bengaluru North, has appointed him as a music teacher, and so the mother-son duo now conduct his class in that campus, too.

It is a great relief for our parents who worry about his future constantly. I already have a permanent job at the Military Engineering Services and am able to look after my wife and toddler daughter, but they worry about what will happen to Ritvik after they are gone. Now that he has found his own niche in the job market, they worry less about him.

The journey so far has been tumultuous; sometimes exciting, sometimes challenging but largely fulfilling. There have been innumerable awards in recognition of our music and God has given us much. A couple of years ago, former President Dr Abdul Kalam paid us a visit at our home and we had the pleasure of singing some of his favourite songs for him. How many normally-abled people would have the good fortune to be able to perform for a former President of the country? But even today, the biggest award for us is the sound of applause from an appreciative audience and the pat on the back, and the hug that we get from our parents after a good performance.

Siddharth G.J.

The sketch compares Siddharth with a diamond that emerges from the dark blocks of charcoal.

He says, 'One word to describe me would be "Fighter".' Hence, a diamond which has gained its qualities after a long, arduous, and an enduring catharsis which brings about a magical transformation to its being, very much akin to the context, and he is looked upon with an awe by the people, a feeling comparable to that of spotting a diamond.

It is not often that a 33-year-old grows to a stature where a former President of the country counts him among his friends. Very few people that age have the breadth of experience, perspective, or maturity to be invited to deliver leadership and motivational lectures at some of the country's most reputed corporate houses and educational institutions. Siddharth G J does all of this and makes it seem like a cakewalk. He is no CEO, MD, or tech-wizard, has no degrees from any prestigious foreign university, and yet, he is a much sought after public speaker, a man whose talks are always met with standing ovations. Siddharth's motivational talks, a heart-warming mix of humour, sarcasm, pathos, and courage pumps up the spirits and morale of leaders who steer the fortunes of multi-million dollar companies. Among Siddharth's legion of admirers is the former President of India, Abdul Kalaam, who calls him 'his friend, the banker from Chennai.' Siddharth also happens to suffer from cerebral palsy and though I had read about the condition, I had never dealt with someone afflicted by it which made me seriously worried while I waited for him to arrive at a five star hotel in one of Bengaluru's sprawling Information Technology Parks. But that is before he stepped out of the elevator like a burst of sunshine, beaming as if he was meeting a long-lost friend.

We walked into the hotel's café for breakfast and instantly, all eyes were on him.

Siddharth's gait and his posture are not like the rest of us and his speech has a slight slur. Most people who don't know about Cerebral Palsy would likely label people with this affliction as mentally retarded but the fact is that this cannot be farther than the truth. The stares didn't seem to bother Siddharth, and we headed straight to a corner table where we settled down, he with his plate of sandwiches and water melon juice and me with a scalding cup of tea. 'I don't drink tea. It is not too good for the system,' he told me. 'I prefer a glass of butter milk because it is soothing for the stomach.' Siddharth did not show any signs of fatigue after an overnight bus trip from Chennai to Bengaluru in what, he told me, was a rickety bus. 'I am used to such things. My mother worries when I undertake such hectic travel but I tell her I am young and able to do this without trouble.'

Siddharth's story is one of amazing grace in the face of life's tough and often, cruel challenges. It is the story of a boy who refused to let anybody pull down his spirit and of a man who today, uses his story and the lessons that he learnt along the way, to inspire and motivate thousands of people.

When I was a little boy, I knew one thing for sure. Every time my younger sister got up to some mischief and got a thrashing from our father, it would be my turn next. Minutes after he had delivered a stinging deterrent on my sister, Seema, Appa would pull me up in the same manner.

Over two decades later, now that I myself have become a father to an infant boy, I would say that it was the biggest gift my parents gave me. They never treated us differently. We were equal in their eyes and their belief that I could grow up to hold my own in this world, made me believe I could do it, too.

Those who know me say that I have done more than just hold my own in what is otherwise a very unequal world for the differently-abled. Over the last few years, I have steadily grown in my career in the banking industry, continuously raised my bar till I became the country's first person with cerebral palsy to be a Certified Documentary Credit Specialist, when, in fact, only just over 54 percent people who appeared for this exam with me, globally, in 2006, made the cut. I am frequently told that my performance at work is not just an inspiration for those like me but that it has also opened doors to meaningful employment for those who have been turned down by potential employers who believed that people with disability cannot cope with the requirements of a work place. I never went to school till the age of 8 and yet I managed to catch up and get a degree in Commerce and a Master's in Economics with over 70 percent marks! Both my amma and my sister say that my story is nothing short of a fairy tale!

For my parents, raising me as an equal was a leap of faith because months after I was born, they realized that their first born was not showing the normal signs of development that other kids of his age showed. I had developed jaundice when I was just 3-days old and the affliction probably was the fall-out of this.

My parents, simple village folk, did not realize that the delay in treating the ailment had worsened my condition. The doctor who was treating me was transferred and by the time the other doctor took over, the damaged was done. While the jaundice was treated, it left in its wake a condition that was to permanently mark me as different from others in the universe. When the doctors finally gave their verdict, the world collapsed around the middle-class couple. Though I had cerebral palsy, they told my parents that I was mentally retarded. Soon, my condition manifested itself and I developed disconnected bodily movements, sometimes contorted facial movements, speech impairment, and poor control on posture.

My condition shattered their life but the couple refused to believe that I was mentally retarded. They knew from the way I responded that I was as intelligent as other infants of the same age, only I looked and behaved differently.

My story could have been similar to that of any post graduate student, had it not been for an attack of cerebral palsy so early on that I did not even get a chance to experience what 'normal' means.

With little clue about raising a kid who was different from others, my parents kept me at home till about the age of 8 till one day, a neighbour introduced them to a school in Bengaluru which, they said, handled children of different abilities.

My life changed overnight under the guidance of able and sensitive teachers. Realizing that they had an intelligent child whose condition did not allow him to write, they taught me to use the typewriter. Some of the teachers tell me today that I took to my lessons like a fish to water. Learning to type with a single finger in one hand , I became a busybody, constantly hammering away at the machine, finishing my homework, and pestering my mom for more work. And when I started doing well in my class, it was a vindication of their effort and their steadfast belief in my abilities.

Much of the credit of my eventful journey goes to my mother, a simple homemaker who devoted most of her time to me, reading out my lessons and keeping my curious mind engaged with stories of kind kings, demons, beautiful princesses, and evil queens. Realizing that I got bored very easily, my father bought me a typewriter at home and that helped me do my studies diligently and kept me occupied. Often, my mother would read out my lessons and I would type them out with great enthusiasm because the typewriter fascinated me.

My parents never left me alone at home. Wherever they went, they took me along and so I never felt I was different or not normal. My younger sister and I were always treated the same by them, and that meant the world to me. They never compared me to her and so I never got a complex or worried about things like why she got to go to school and had friends while I had to stay at home.

At the Spastic Society School in Bengaluru I became a favourite of the teachers and even though I had no understanding of it, my hard work earned me a double promotion from upper KG. But all the good times came to an abrupt halt when my father was transferred to Chennai. I was heartbroken when I was told that I would have to leave the school and my beloved teachers and go to a totally unfamiliar city. Thankfully for me, my parents found Vidya Sagar, a school for spastic children, where another set of teachers took over my progress. Here too, I excelled in my studies—when they realized that I was ahead of my class and capable of much more, they allowed me to telescope 6th, 7th and 8th grade and to complete it in eighteen months flat. When I continued to do well in class, they decided one day that I was ready to join a mainstream school. Vidya Sagar had come to be my little world and once again, I found my life disrupted. Going to a regular school—Boston Matriculation—in 9th grade was my first step to being part of the world in which everybody else lived. It was challenging—I was unable to cope with the work load, did not understand how to make friends with my class mates, and was miserable because of a self-imposed pressure to not let down my people or disappoint my own expectations from me. My parents never expected anything from me. They let me be the way I was but I was and continue to be driven to excel.

My need to excel eventually pushed me to work so hard that I scored 80 percent marks in the class 10th grade board exams and 90 percent in the 12th grade board exams, despite the fact that the scribe that the school allocated to write my exam was not well versed with subjects or even languages. At many points, I had to explain the simplest facts to my writer and dictate each answer, word to word. Try dictating papers like accounts, mathematics, economics, or computer science and that too, to a scribe who could not understand English!

As it turned out, this was the least of the challenges I had to face. When I applied for admission to the Swami Vivekananda College, I got the shock of my life when I was refused admission despite my academic records. They looked at me and concluded I would not be able to cope with the curriculum in college. It was only after my school and my parents stepped in and convinced the college that I would add value to their institute, that they relented and admitted me to a Bachelor of Commerce degree. Next stop for me was the Loyola College where I joined to complete an MA in Economics. My heart was initially set on doing a Masters in Social Work but I was flatly refused admission because no one believed that I would be able to cope with social work, given the extent of my disability. My disability certificate says I am 70 percent disabled but nobody knew that this fact challenged me enough to make sure that I would always score over 70 percent in every major exam that I wrote. A lot of people were astonished when I scored a 74 percent in B. Com and 77 percent in MA Economics, but not me. I had worked towards it. The years in college were tough as was the time immediately after my MA when I was rejected at one job interview after another. The initial period in the regular school was also the time when my spirits flagged and I would weave in and out of depression. In addition to the fact that I was already floundering with the work load and could not write, my innate shyness proved to be debilitating because that kept me from reaching out to make friends. To make matters worse, my classmates in school and college, much like the rest of the world, did not know how to approach or interact with a person with disability. I struggled with finding acceptance and yearned for a kindred spirit with whom I could share my life. Sadly, that never happened till I finished my education. Today, I can say that parents and teachers need to figure out how to make sure that differently-abled children go to mainstream schools because that is the only way the two can understand each other and be sensitive to each other's situation. Stung by repeated rejections at various job interviews, I raged at the unfairness of it all, griping, grumbling, and complaining endlessly about my situation. I was angry most of the time back then, very, very angry, and the more the world's rejection hurt me the more I would vent my frustration on my family, especially my mother and Seema. My rants continued till one day, I realized that my constant sadness and anger was putting too much pressure on my body and making me ill. With cerebral palsy, my brain and bodily movements are already not coordinated. My constant stress was making that condition worse and I was falling ill often. Self-awareness came late but I am glad it came because it made me introspect and take charge of my life and change the way I lived in the world. It did not happen overnight. It was a long process that took me some eight years after my 12th grade, before my mind finally stabilized. Along the way, I realized that my anger and unhappiness was also burdening my parents. The only person who did not succumb to my ranting was my sister. I picked on her when I was angry, we fought all the time but she was my wonderful companion. Seema made me look at things from another perspective and that calmed me down sometimes.

The renewed focus on life also possibly helped me focus even more on academics and I had graduated with 100 percent in management accountancy and done well in computer science, both of which proved priceless in my future career.

All the anger, the sadness at being rejected continually by employers who paid no attention to my credentials but focused, instead, on my disability, changed the day I got my first job.

In 2005, I attended an interview at ABN AMRO Central Enterprises Services Pvt Ltd and I went with very little hope because of all the previous rejections. This time, however, I struck gold. Instead of the cynicism and rejection that I expected, I found an interview panel that allowed me to talk uninterrupted. I spoke about myself, my hard work, my achievements in school, my struggles, and about my interests. They let me speak without interrupting for 45 minutes which was a long time for someone who was used to being rejected within minutes. It was almost as if they were happy to know me! At the end of the interview, I walked home with a job offer in the bank's Document Checking section of the Letter of Credit Department, as an Officer Trainee. In that one moment, every single tear that I had shed over the last few years, all the sadness, and the feeling of inadequacy disappeared. I was on top of the world. I was very proud because this was something I had earned for myself, without any recommendations or favours from anyone.

At my new job, success followed and I forged ahead, clearing the Trade Finance and other courses before recertifying myself as a Certified Documentary Credit Specialist in 2010. A few years later, I moved on from that job and today, I work with IndusInd Bank Ltd as a manager.

Alongside, my fascination for computers and technology had kept me busy researching stuff online. Hungry for friends and social interaction, I explored social networking sites , reaching out to people on-line, and it was Facebook that finally proved to be the turning point of my life. A Facebook friend chanced upon a video about me that a friend had shared and he was so intrigued by my story that he sought me out for a meeting. That chance meeting was to prove to be the turning point of my life because he was also one of the organizers of the influential TEDx Chennai and wanted to put me on a prestigious platform to talk about my journey.

My tryst with public speaking began at the launch of a book authored by this friend's school-going daughter, where I was invited to speak as a special guest. The book was about the about the virtue of counting one's blessings rather than complaining about what one does not have, and when I narrated the story of my own life, many in the audience cried. When it was over, my friend said that I was just the right speaker to connect with a large audience of thinkers and influencers.

A month after that, I was on a stage at TEDx Chennai, telling an audience of some 250 people about my life's ups and downs, and my eventual victory over my circumstances. And when I finished, the audience surprised me with a standing ovation. The journey that began with the first TEDx talk has now become the foundation on which I base my journey as a motivational speaker. . In the three years since the first talk, I have delivered around a hundred talks at educational institutions, corporate houses, gatherings of HR managers etc. I love it because it allows me to be me, to laugh at myself, and to tell the world about the way I look at the world.

The credit for everything I have achieved in life goes to my amma, appa, and my teachers who transformed me with their love and taught me the virtue of patience. For years in school and college, I was angry with the world and vented my frustrations on my mother but instead of saying an unkind word to me she continued to devote all her attention on making my life easy. In many ways, she made me who I am. Her patience eventually taught me to be more patient and even though it was tough, I was able to convince myself that how I lived my life was my choice. I could rage and crib about it, and be unhappy, or I could accept my situation and find happiness in it. I chose the latter and have never regretted it in the last few years.

Along the way, I have learnt some precious life lessons that allow me to live a content life. My parents taught me to take life as it comes. 'Don't worry about what will happen tomorrow or years from now. Whatever happens, we will deal with it,' is their constant refrain. Together, we have weathered lot of storms and struggles, and nothing worries us anymore. I have learnt the merit in keeping life simple and uncluttered. I don't waste energy thinking about the future. Sometimes, the worries come sneaking in on my mind but my parent's philosophy of not worrying about the future helps me overcome my anxieties. Often, when I talk about my life on various platforms, my mind goes back to my initial struggles and I find myself weighed down but thankfully, it is temporary. I allow myself to go back to the past but now I find that the mind automatically comes back to the present, without effort. Living a positive life calls for tremendous control over the mind and I have managed that after a hard struggle.

I have always been driven to do my best and to me, that means doing everything whole heartedly, not just because it has to be done but because it makes me and those around me happy. My parents rarely attend my speaking events because the story of my struggle makes them emotional, but one of their biggest joys is the fact that I have made so many strides in my life when, in fact, life gave me no chance at all. Along the way, I have been able to understand that being the best is not what matters in life but inculcating the right intention and attitude is everything. I know I can never be the best or even one amongst the best in anything but knowing I have done things whole heartedly is the most important for me.

I have also realized that my problems are mine alone and I cannot keep passing them on or burdening anyone with them. I have realized that nobody wants to be with a person who is constantly morose and I have decided to accept that, and adopt a happy stance for myself.

When I stopped cribbing and complaining about my life to my parents and to my teachers at Vidya Sagar, it was because I did not want to burden or disappoint them. It was not that the world's rejection did not hurt. It did, every day, but I chose to not to let it affect me anymore.

Often, I am asked what my dreams are and I say that I don't dream. Life has taught me not to dream. I live each day to the fullest and that, in itself, is a dream, isn't it? For the last three years, my talks at various campuses have given me a sense of purpose and meaning. Every day, I find myself evolving as a speaker. I still remember the day after my first speech at TEDx, my story was on the front page of The Hindu, and it was uplifting and exhilarating. The most rewarding thing in my life today is my ability to talk to people and someway motivate and inspire them. For someone who had no friends till the age of 25, today I have more friends that I can keep count of. I have 1,900, friends on Facebook and that never ceases to surprise me. They are fans and well-wishers who want to be connected to me and I am glad they are part of my journey. When I was making strides in my job at the bank, the then President of India, Abdul Kalam, who happened to read about me in a newspaper, dropped in to meet me when he was in Chennai. I was lucky to have met him a few more times in the last few years when I was receiving some awards, but I never imagined that I had left an impression on his mind. Sometime ago, at an event in Chennai, Kalam Sir spotted me in the audience and told the audience that he had seen his 'friend, the banker from Chennai,' and that he was glad I was there! It was definitely a very special moment for me. I am told that he often quotes me when he is delivering motivational talks at various platforms.

Some three years ago, I had told my sister and my mom that I wanted to go out and talk about my life, and they had been taken aback and asked me what I thought I had to talk about and who would come listen to me. Today, they pull my leg saying I am a celebrity speaker.

What keeps me going is my ambition to go out and talk to even more people. I love interacting with people, and the more people I touch with my talks, the happier I feel. My work is close to my heart, too. I know what people think of the differently-abled people. I have seen it, felt it, lived with people's assumption that a disabled person cannot do anything in life. When I go to work every day and fulfil my responsibilities, I know I am a contributing member of the organization and that always brings a sense of achievement.

The more I faced the outside world, the more I realized that it is easier for me to try and understand the world rather than to expect the world to understand me. I have learnt never to waste my energies in analysing people because it is not beneficial in anyway. And I never invest my time in planning for the future because that is not in our control at all.

My job gave me the opportunity to meet people, something I never had before, but the irony was that when I finally got to meet people every day at work, I was not ready for it. I did not want to meet people or make friends because I was used to loneliness. I struggled to get over the instinct to keep to myself but gradually, having to interact with my colleagues led to friendships that I least expected.

Initially, it was not easy and I required a lot of courage because I was not used to having people around me. Today, I realize that there are good people who will go beyond themselves to understand people like me and bring meaning into our lives. I have been blessed with good people who have helped me move forward in my career, creating opportunities for me while keeping my limitations in mind. I was collapsing under the strain of the cynicism, the disbelief that society carries about the abilities of differently-abled people, but I survived only because there were a lot of people who believed in me and treated me the same way as they treated other employees. These, to my mind, are true leaders. Even today, I stay in touch with each of the people who made contributions in my life and gave me a chance to prove my abilities. When the interview panel at RBS realized that I was good at mind-work, they gave me a job in trade finance which required a lot of analytical abilities. My job with documentation checking is challenging, fulfilling, and taps my abilities to the fullest.

If there is just one word to describe me, that would be 'fighter'. I am a fighter on the outside but soft inside. Anything that is humane touches me because only human beings can reach out and make another person feel relevant. I look for genuineness in people because that is such a precious quality to have. I count myself lucky because I have come across a few genuine people who have touched my life.

A couple of years ago, I got married to a wonderful woman who is now a very understanding companion to me. It was love at first sight for me. Choosing her as my life partner was the first independent decision I have taken. We are now proud parents of a toddler and I am so thrilled that I have one more person in my life to love. When he runs around the house, it is something I never could do but I like to think I am living my childhood through him.

When I am not at work or on a speaking assignment, I spend

time at home with my mom and family. I remember the years my mother devoted to me and I want to do that for her now. When my sister got married a few years ago and mom felt lonely, I stayed at home a lot, even if I was simply sleeping all day! I think just being around for the people who love you is very important. Today, I know that problems are a part and parcel of life. Everybody has them but how we deal with them is what decides who we become. My biggest challenge was accepting myself the way I am and it was a long and painful struggle but in the end I did it.

Today, I compare myself to no one because I am unique in my own way. Wanting to be like someone else will defeat the purpose of me being Siddharth. I want to be no one else but me.

Syndeep Rao

The sketch is a wrap that personifies Sundeep as a stand-up comedian. The bulb can be seen as an idea that struck him, to take up this profession, also as much needed light in the darkness. The black background is symbolic of his despair and anguish while growing up and also subtly indicates the loss of eye-sight. But the bulb again brings about the sense of triumph over the disability to the foreground. Also, in the sketch one could view Sundeep as a torchbearer who has the ability to laugh at his own challenges and thus, holds a mirror at the mainstream society.

'The inability to laugh at life's problems, challenges, and inadequacies is a disability in itself!'

Sundeep Rao is partially blind but if you were to go by his definition of disability, he would be the fittest amongst us, considering that he has made a living out of laughing at the problems and challenges that life has thrown at him. Sundeep has the rare privilege of being able to make a career out of his passion: stand-up comedy.

It is not easy to be born blind but to slowly have your vision fade away is far worse. Thankfully, Sundeep saw the light at the end of the tunnel and decided that he would not disappear into the background just because he couldn't see. He has played golf, cricket, and basketball, written radio jingles, and drunk himself silly but when all of that was over, he decided to use his experiences of growing up as a visually impaired person in India to bring some laughter in the lives of people.

When this cool dude walks on to the stage flaunting his earring and smart threads, the audience collectively holds its breath because they know for sure that before the evening winds up, many of them will have become the butt of his razor sharp wit. And, they will have fallen off their chairs, laughing.

Sundeep has done over a 150 stand- up comedy acts over the last few years and his audience still can't have enough of him. Meeting up with him was one of the rare occasions when I forgot my many deadlines and the things on my to-do list. I was just content sitting at a restaurant table, laughing my guts out, as he kept up a stream of tongue-in-cheek one-liners about the life and times of a blind visually impaired stand-up comedian.

My journey of self-discovery began on an eventful evening in January 2013 at the imposing Chowdiah Memorial Hall in Bengaluru. I had been there many times before with my mother, attending musical evenings and plays but this was different. This evening, I was going on stage with a couple of my friends, with Full Circle, a stand-up comedy act which could make or break me. I was going in with everything that was unconventional , including the name of my group, 'The Polished Bottoms' and yet, we had sold 700 out of the 1000 seats at the Chowdia and that, in itself, put the fear of God into me. If this show fell on its face, there would be no place for me to hide.

The show started with my partners, Praveen Kumar, Sanjay Manaktala, and Shyam Bhat, going in first and I could see (well, not really), people were lapping it up. I walked on stage for the closing act, my knees trembling and my heartbeat roaring in my ears. When it ended, the applause from the audience was sweet music to my ears and when they got on their feet to give me a standing ovation, it was like a cherished dream had come true.

I knew I was funny; I had been getting laughs from the audience for two years, I had done almost fifty shows at some reputed places including comedy stores such as Laugh Factory and done over thirty shows for corporate events, but this was different. I had forever been in awe of performances at the Chowdiah and here I was, being applauded by a 700 strong audience. I had finally found my space. I was, finally, a stand up comedian of repute and people would now laugh with me instead of at me. When I walked off stage, I had tears in my eyes. I was a happy man and I felt like I had delivered my first baby!

You might not think so but laughter is serious business and for me, it had been a rocky road to the Chowdiah. Ever heard of a blind stand-up comedian? That was me and I had never thought my life would take such a twist! Not that I was ever deterred by my situation from trying out anything new.

At the age of 8–9, when I started gradually losing my vision due to juvenile macular degeneration, a condition that normally affects an ageing population, I was very angry with life and I took out all of that rage on my parents. I threw tantrums and I became a very rebellious child, blaming them for my misfortune. My mom was my scapegoat because she was the one who was always around and she would take it all without a murmur. Her stand was simple—I was her baby and she would stand by me, no matter what.

But eventually, that rage settled and I went back to being the active, pleasant child that I was. My mother told me early on that I could either be sad and sit around doing nothing or have a life that I wanted. She made sure that I went to a normal school where I did everything that other children of my age did. I used to run the 100 metres, 200 metres, and 400 metres track events, and take part in the long jump and high jump. Doing my lessons were difficult because I could not read much as I only had peripheral vision and that too, partial, but my mother made up for that by helping out with my studies, patiently taking down notes and reading out to me.

Mom pushed me to do other things as well, such as playing the piano and today, it is one of the things that I turn to when I am stressed or when I want to relax. Tennis, cricket, volleyball, basketball, I did all of that, sometimes getting hit on the face with the ball, but nothing deterred me. For five years, I learnt golf and at around the age of 14, I thought I was good enough in the game and even signed up for a golfing contest. No one was surprised when I came last in the contest but I got the most applause because they appreciated my courage to be there on that golf course despite my impaired vision. I still love sports and if I were given the choice, I would pick tennis over spending time working out at the gym.

I believe that things happen in our life sometimes that impact us deeply, change our world view, and remain with us for a long time. At the age of 16, when I was in the 10th grade, I won an extremely competitive election to become the sports captain of my school. My euphoria over the fact that every single vote had been cast in my favour was short-lived when the teacher announced that I could not be the sports captain because I was blind. It was a terrible disappointment and my mind kept posing this big WHY to myself. That's also the time I realized there's no point in competing in any mainstream activity because however eligible I was, there would always be another authority who would point out to my disability and say I was not capable of doing this, that, or the other.

Maybe, at a subconscious level, this was what nudged me

in the direction of a more unconventional goal, career, and passion. I will never know...

But even though that is a bad memory from my teenaged years, I have great memories, too, of the kindness that I was surrounded with when my world seemed to be fading away bit by bit. In those days, my life was an endless round of hospital visits, CT scans, opinions, second opinions, and all kinds of interns pushing and poking in my eyes to figure out what was wrong. One day, my parents took me to Sankara Nethralaya in Madras where I met Dr Badrinath, a kind man who won my heart by simply saying, 'Come on son, things will be okay, you're a good boy.' To everyone else, they might have been just words, but for me, it was the difference between despair and hope because around that time, all I had around me were people discussing my condition in hushed voices. I was a 9-year-old boy who was terrified and Dr Badrinath was the lone man who propped me up during a dark period in my life.

The year I turned 18, I had my first melt down. That was the time my friends were starting to get their driving licenses, buying cars and motorcycles and I realized I would never get to drive at all. That was the first time I broke down and had a royal crying session, bemoaning my misfortune, and cursing my blindness. That was the point my dad offered to buy me a Go-kart. In fact, he called up a manufacturer and asked if he could buy a Go-kart for his visually impaired son. Of course, we never bought one but the fact that he wanted to do it was enough for me and I love him for it. I did drive a car eventually, from the bus stop to my house which was five minutes away but even that stopped when I crashed into a stationary jeep one night.

The good thing is that today, I don't remember the days when my eye sight was good. In fact, I have made my peace with the things happening in my life and can talk about my blindness and poke fun at myself, like I do in my solo act, Out Of Sight.

The story of that act itself started a couple of years ago, during the time when I was utterly bored with life, thanks to successive job assignments that did little for either my morale or bank balance. I had worked in an advertising agency writing jingles, had joined an internet radio station where I had thought I'd get to do my own show, but ended up doing terrible radio ads on air, and I worked in the internal communications department of an IT firm. Sadly, none of them appealed to me.

Around this time, a friend of mine told me about comedian Vir Das and his 'hamateur nights' where anybody could go in and take the mic to put up a comic act in a two-minute slot. 'Why don't you do a two-minute spot?' he said to me because I used to be the clown in our group of friends. I used to watch a lot of stand-up comedy shows by the likes of George Carlin, watch Mitch Hedberg and Eddie Izzard and when I saw this opportunity, I thought I would give it a try. Just for fun, not knowing this would be my career and my passion in the years to come.

My first shot at comedy was more like a nightmare. I had written a two-minute skit with great enthusiasm and delivered it with all my heart. Sadly, nobody in the audience saw the humour. Ditto the second and the third time. Nobody understood the stuff I was referring to in my act. I walked onto the stage the fourth time and spoke about the state of Bengaluru's roads and cracked lame jokes about drunk people and suddenly people in the audience were nodding their heads, laughing, and clapping. I had cracked it! All the fear in my mind disappeared and I realized I loved the attention and that I wanted to be on stage more than just the two minutes that I did, every now and then.

My opportunity arrived in 2010 when the owner of a restaurant which I used to frequent asked me if I would like to put up a comedy show there. I was terrified at the thought because all I had done until then were these small slots. Coincidentally, I ran into Sanjay Manaktala, a friend of mine who had moved from the US on a project with his company. We met at a restaurant where there was an open mic happening and we realized that both of us were interested in doing snap comedy. The result of that meeting was our first ever twosome, Snap Night, in which I performed for twenty-three very long minutes at Bacchus. We took everything seriously for this debut—we got ourselves a funny name, put up posters, summoned friends and family, made sure the place was full, and that we looked like really cool comedians.

It was a small beginning but somehow, the success of that night made me confident that I could do it, that I could anchor a comedy night for a longer time. That was over three years ago and when I look back, it seems almost unreal that I pulled it off for the longest time without ever letting my audience know that I was partially blind. I did not want to be pitied or stereotyped as the blind guy who does comedy. I knew I could be funny without or even despite my blindness. In the past three years, I've done every kind of joke, but there's been nothing related to my vision.

That, in itself, was terrifying in the beginning. For almost one year, I would rehearse to the point where I knew every word in my act. I would know exactly how many steps to take to get to the centre of the stage, knew exactly where my props were kept, and knew how many men and women were seated in the front row. It was scary because so many things could go wrong. I managed, nevertheless, but the flip side was that my act sounded too scripted, and irrespective of who the audience was, I wouldn't change the jokes. But as I got more confident on stage, I realized that sometimes you need to adapt, take a chance, and try something you have never tried before in style of delivery or body language. It was a risk worth taking and today, I am more confident of getting into an act without everything scripted in advance.

Sometime last year, I realized that I was now ready to talk to my audiences about my blindness. My solo, Out Of Sight, took a long time to come but this act is, in some ways, a coming of age for me and it is all about my personal trials and tribulations, as a blind person in our country.

For years, I have tried to travel without ever asking for help but now, when I get into an airport to board a flight, I don't hesitate to ask for assistance. What follows is hilarious. The other day I told the lady at the check-in at Bengaluru airport that I was blind and needed assistance to get to the flight. She promptly offered me a wheelchair! In India, nobody understands partial impairment. If you are blind, they need to see your cane. I have learnt to get around this with humour. When they ask me why I have no cane to show that I am blind, I promptly tell them that I don't have one because I can't find it!

In a way, talking about my blindness is liberating, almost therapeutic. I can talk about anything at all, including the dangers of a blind man going out on a date. I end up with the wrong person- sometimes even a long haired man instead of a woman with raven locks!

I think stand-up comedy came to me as a defence mechanism because I realized humour is the easiest thing to diffuse a situation. If someone picks on you, puts you down, or makes a hurtful comment, it is just easier to just use comedy to lighten up the situation as opposed to beating up the person.

In the past, I have been aggressive and gotten into fights when malicious comments were made about my condition but now I know that comedy is a lot easier if you crack a joke. Even if it is a bad joke, no one gets hurt at the end of it. Before stand-up comedy, alcohol was my retreat from uncomfortable situations but I realized after a point that it was unhealthy. I was drinking and then getting up on some random stage, taking the karaoke or microphone and making a clown of myself till one day I realized how disrespectful I was being to myself. I wanted to be on stage but not as a drunken clown. That was when stand-up comedy became a life-saver. Today, when I do stand-up comedy, I'm not being a clown; I'm actually being respected for what I'm saying. When I go up on stage, talking about things which upset me, the audience laughs at the jokes but they also identify with it because these are things that upset them as well. That is the point of comedy, not laughing at somebody's misfortune or looks.

Each of us reach a turning point in life when all the familiar, old things change. For me, there were two things. One was going abroad, to the UK and to the US, for my studies. It was one of the most exciting phases of my life. I don't know how much Sociology I studied in the US, but away from the protective care of my family, I learnt to fend for myself. Unlike the Indian educational system, the Americans focus on learning that is analytical. It was tough initially to present what I had studied, rationally explain it, and defend my position from what I had understood about the subject. It was very different from the Indian system of rote learning. It was also one of the most amazing experiences of my life because I became an independent and sensible person who could defend myself with confidence.

Every parent wants to protect their child but looking back, I know from my own experience that the best way you can protect a child is by sending him/her to take on the world, in the best way they can. Because if you keep the child close to you, that child's going to be like a snail, stuck in his shell, and unable to handle anything independently. I have learnt that the world is not going to wait for you; the world is going to move on because they have other things to do with their time.

One of the other things that changed my life is my discovery of audio books. I was gifted a couple of audio books a few years ago and I was hooked, not just because I got to know about some fine stories but because I was fascinated by the way the narrators used their voice to convey so many things . The inflection in their voice and the impact they have on a story by simply changing their pitch or intonation taught me a lot that I now use in my comedy act. I became an ardent follower of audio books in my early 20s and eight years later, I am at a stage when I go through at least four books a month. If I ever get my sight back, my dream job is to be a narrator for audio books.

I might be a great comic but my life has not always been always bright and cheerful. but whenever I have faltered there has been someone who has pulled me up and put me back on my feet . My mother has been the person for me, the selfless soul who sat up entire days drawing lines on sheets of paper so that I could write on a straight line. She converted my lessons into audio so I could learn by listening to my lessons. She would go to museums and other places so that my history projects would be faultless. My elder sister is a source of endless strength and then, there is this wonderful girl who is completely blind and is an 8th grade piano player who happens to also be doing a triple major at Yale. She is incredibly inspiring, humble, and full of beans. She has pulled me out of my blue funks on several occasions.

Today, I have come to a point when I find my own life inspiring. There are times when I get disheartened looking at other people who are more successful, other comedians getting more corporate shows, more recognition but then I ask myself, 'Where were you five years ago when you came back from the US? You were drinking too much, being obnoxious. Just four years ago, you were getting on stage for the first time and were petrified of doing a two-minute slot. In 2010, you started a full-fledged comedy night on your own and today, you are doing your own solo act , talking about your life for an entire hour, and opening up to strangers about your flaws and your experiences as a disabled person.'

I am very different today from the person I used to be. My parents used to think that I was just fooling around when

I initially started doing the two-minute open mics but one evening, they came in for one of my shows and they realized I am actually not a bad stand-up comedian at all . Today, they are among my biggest supports.

There are times when I wake up and don't feel funny. Some days, I have a really terrible show and I don't get a single guest laughing, even when I think I really deserved it and then I wonder if I have made a wrong decision in following the path of comedy. But within the deepest corner of my heart I know that comedy is what helped me find myself.

Because I always wanted to please people, because I thought I'd done something wrong by going blind, I ended up being a perpetually apologetic person, saying, 'Oh, I'm so sorry', even if I tripped on someone's foot. Considering that I was blind, it was the other person who should have apologized but I ended up saying sorry for everything. If the same thing were to happen today, I'm more likely to say, 'Excuse me, your leg is in the way and I am the blind person around here!' I'm less apologetic, less keen to please people. I'm more of myself now. Being a stand-up comedian has really helped me discover who I am.

Today, I have an opinion of my own and a lot of self-worth. I am at peace with the fact that some people might like me, others might not. I don't have to always be the comedian in the group anymore because I am not starved of attention. I get a lot of that on stage. I get recognized for being a person who has a valid and funny opinion on things. But more than the comedy aspect of it, my blindness has made me a better person. Angry, maybe frustrated sometimes, maybe unreasonable sometimes but also someone who has learnt to be humble and sensitive.

Right now, I'm living my dream. It's a frustrating dream, it's a sad dream, it's a nightmare at times but I still I don't feel like waking up, because it is my dream. And I like the joke in it.

Sunil Desai

Sunil has been perceived and portrayed as a tree with many black lines that shape up its trunk and branches, subtle foliage, and a deep shade underneath! The many black lines appear dry, life-less, lack movement, and stand still...much like the paralysed body of Sunil. Yet, the first outward glance is outwitted by foliage around it (symbolic to the spirit of life that embodies Sunil) and its protective shade indicates the love and compassion with which Sunil has brought about a social initiative—The Care Takers!

In the crowded by-lanes of Karelibaug in Baroda, Sunil Desai is a familiar figure. Most days, he arrives at the local market on his four-wheeler, taking his time to choose the freshest vegetables and chatting with the vegetable vendors who know his and his family's favoured vegetables and fruits because he has been their loyal customer for over a decade now. Desai will also go to the neighbourhood 'kirana wallah' to pick up groceries for his wife, Darshana, and he will have met half a dozen friends in the neighbourhood to exchange pleasantries with before he heads home as dusk falls. Along the way, if he happens to notice a traffic policeman missing from his post at busy intersections, he will call up the traffic authorities and request them to send someone over to resolve a nasty traffic jam. Not a bad routine for a man who is paralysed and has spent his life as a quadriplegic for close to twenty years now, completely dependent on his battery-operated wheelchair that has given him wings and a new life.

At 34 years of age, I was on top of the world. I had a great job as the area sales manager of a well-known electronics goods company. I had a loving family, a house of my own, and prospects of further advancement in my workplace. I felt life could not be better for me. When I stepped into the luxury bus that would take me to Rajkot, where I had an important business meeting on that fateful day in 1994, I had no idea that journey would result in the end of my life as I knew it and become the beginning of a journey that was overwhelmingly difficult initially, but would bring me fulfilment eventually.

It was going to be a long journey and I was longing for a comfortable seat so I could rest myself. As soon as I got onto the bus, I asked for a change of seat, insisting on a seat at the front of the bus so that I got additional leg space to stretch out during the journey. Little did I know that decision would inexorably alter the course of my future. A few hours later, my bus had a head-on collision with a tanker on a lonely stretch of the Limdi-Bagodra highway near Rajkot, the impact killing several people in the bus, including the passenger sitting next to me. I was barely alive, my limbs were caught in the mangled remains of the bus, and my life changed forever.

Somewhere in the midst of all the chaos of people trying to rescue passengers from the bus, I realized that something was seriously wrong with my body. I had no sensation at all and other than my neck, I found my body had become a dead weight that I could not move. Doctors at a small hospital where I was taken said that my nervous system and spinal cord had been severely damaged in the accident and I would have to be moved to a bigger hospital in Rajkot immediately. I insisted that I wanted to be shifted to Vadodara where my family was but the doctors said I was in dire straits and would possibly not live beyond 24–72 hours if I did not get urgent medical attention. I stood my ground and asked for a tempo which drove me to Ahmedabad where I was put in hospital. What followed was a series of surgeries with the doctors trying hard to rescue me but their verdict, eventually, spelt the death knell for my hopes and aspirations. I would never be able to move again. From flying high with my head in the clouds, my life was cruelly, abruptly, brought crashing down. In medical terms, I was now a quadriplegic and would spend my life on a wheelchair.

It was a period of desolation for me and inexplicable trauma for my family. I had two little girls who had to be educated and married, I had an old father to support, and my wife was shattered that the head of her family was now completely dependent on the family to look after him. But if anyone thought that my wife would collapse under the weight of the burden on her shoulders, they were to be proved wrong. Over the next few years, she used every ounce of her strength and willpower to give me my life back. We visited countless hospitals and tried every alternate therapy available, in the hope that my lifeless body could regain its strength back. After spending

Rs 15 lakh on all of this, we knew all our efforts were in vain. I would never walk again.

For me, those initial months after the accident were just a series of days when I lay on a bed in our home when all around me, people spoke in hushed tones about my condition. But at least I got to see my friends and family who came to visit and spent time around me chatting and trying to keep me cheerful and distracted from the fact that I was now a cripple. But slowly the number of visitors came down to a trickle and one day I realized, not a single person had come to visit. Suddenly, I felt the terror of being all alone in a room and trapped on bed for the rest of my life. Some days, I shouted and screamed in frustration, some days I wept alone in bed while my family got busy with their daily chores, and eventually, I sunk into a deep quagmire of depression. Then, one day, out of nowhere, my old spirit kicked in and I decided that only I had the power to put the life back in my lifeless body. I decided that day that I would no longer be helpless and dependent because then the world would forget me and I was nowhere nearing giving up on my life yet. I told myself that it was time to stop living in the past because I was letting that ruin my present and my future. I told myself sternly that it was time to take control of my life, face my reality, and accept it. God has given me many gifts and I was ready to use them for a larger purpose. I told myself that my physical body was crippled but my mind was alive and free and I would use it to live the rest of my life fruitfully.

Three months after the accident, I started off my first fledgling venture, using the services of engineers, and setting up a business of servicing air conditioners, refrigerators, and televisions. My long years in the industry helped me because I knew the business inside-out. It was not a lot of money—I gave 70 percent of the fee to the engineer who attended the calls and kept 30 percent for myself. But it was a beginning. I continued the business for over two years but gave up eventually when large consumer electronics firms put up their own servicing network and people switched to using those rather than stand-alone service providers.

I went through another bad patch that lasted for almost six years. I was back to feeling useless and like a burden. I had a restless, very active mind that was struggling to break free from the confines of my lifeless body. My mind ran helter-skelter, trying to figure out ways to escape the misery in which I found myself. And from the hours of endless dialogue that went on inside my head, there emerged an idea that need urgent implementing. I realized how completely helpless and hopeless a person becomes when he/she does not have a support system or a caretaker to understand their needs. My family had helped me every inch of the way—my life is a team effort today with even my father chipping in to help me take on each day. After the huge costs incurred for my surgeries, we had no money to appoint full-time help to look after me so they decided to do it themselves, taking turns to attend to me. I thought of the thousands of people who had no support system like I had and my mind started racing ahead of me because, suddenly, I knew what I wanted to do with the rest of my life. I wanted to make the life of those like me happier and more comfortable. I wanted to start a support and care service for the old, the ailing, and the helpless.

My family was overjoyed at the change in my spirit. They were the ones who had borne the brunt of my anger, depression, and mood swings but none of them, not my wife, my old father, or my daughter had ever said an unkind word to me in the decade I spent whining about my fate.

It was an outrageous idea for someone who himself was immobile and 100 percent dependent but somehow, my friends and my family, who had known me when I was a bundle of energy during my better days, were gripped with the idea. They, themselves, had known the pain I had gone through as a dependent and they knew exactly what goes on in the minds of those trapped in helplessness.

The idea of Care-Taker, the helping institute that I set up almost nine years ago, germinated from my own helplessness but today, it has brought hope and help to hundreds of people in the state of Gujarat and other parts of the country. It started with a small advertisement that I placed in the newspaper, on the auspicious day of my father's birthday, calling for applications from people who wanted to train to be care-givers and get job placements immediately. Admittedly, not all of the people who applied and came to our home for the interview were the kind of people I was looking for. The first batch of men and women who I selected displayed the quality of empathy that I was looking for. Through my own experience I knew that the worst thing for a patient or an invalid is for someone to look after him/her without being sensitive to their feelings. More than the pain of our physical injury, what hurts is the pain of feeling like a burden on our loved ones.

With a modest capital that my friends loaned me, I was back

in business, having employed a dozen men and women who were in need of employment and were willing to work hard for it. My wheelchair became my work table and, with the help of a mobile phone, a head set, and an earplug connected to it that helped me receive calls, I was ready for the next leg of my career. This time, my wife and my father were my executive assistants, helping me conduct interviews, putting the logistics in place, and organizing for my new recruits to undergo the necessary training. With my understanding that care-givers have to be loving, compassionate, and empathetic, I had long conversations with the recruits to emphasise the importance of inculcating those qualities in themselves. And when they had assimilated that, we sent them out to train in patient care—how to lift an invalid, bathe, and feed him/her—and in physiotherapy and acupressure to relieve pain or spasm.

When I was convinced that my first batch of employees were ready with all the necessary skills, I put out my second advertisement, this time saying that we were in the business of providing care for the old, the invalid, and for children. I must confess even I was not prepared for the response. Within days of the advertisement appearing, we were inundated with calls and my wife had a tough time handling the demand that came in from as far as the United States where children of ageing or invalid parents led busy lives. These were people who had great jobs and plenty of money but they lived in guilt over their inability to come back to India and look after their parents. My service was a boon to many of these people.

When some of my early clients realized that I, myself, was a quadriplegic, there were some initial doubts about how efficient this service would be, but when I pointed out that this gave me a deep insight into the care that an invalid needs, they were convinced. And it is this very fact that sets us apart from other organizations that offer care services. Over the years, Care-Taker has largely grown through word-of-mouth-publicity and through referrals from clients themselves. It is not unusual for one satisfied client to refer our organization to family and friends who find themselves in need of quality care for invalids or children. Today I have some 250 caregivers who are looking after the needs of an equal number of invalids and I have a swelling bank of caregivers who can step in whenever required.

If, in the immediate aftermath of the accident, I had thought that my life was finished and that I would have to live a life of dependency and misery, then the last few years of my life has been nothing short of a miracle. With the strength of a loving family beside me and with a couple of wheelchairs—one of which I have adapted to suit the needs of my body—I have reinvented myself and found new meaning to my existence. If my life before the accident was, in some ways, self-serving, my new life is very different. My pain has opened my eyes to the suffering of others in this world. I know today, that the most precious thing of all is the company and the support of loving people around you. Money means nothing at all if there is nobody to share your ups and downs with. Often, I get calls from clients who have more money than they can ever spend in their life but don't have a single person to reach out to in times of need or to even share a conversation with. Today, I find my fulfilment by reaching out to my clients—I visit some of them on a designated day to chat with them and I can't tell you how these visits suddenly transform their drab days. I am available at all times to them or their families on the phone. Caring for an invalid is exhausting, physically and emotionally, and I often talk to the families, and counsel them about various facets of patient care.

Sometimes, I think that the accident and my disability have been a blessing in disguise. They changed a selfish man into someone who is now more compassionate and giving. Setting up Care-Taker gave my own life a direction and sense of purpose. Today, there is a sense of achievement and also fulfilment because I bring comfort and relief from pain into the lives of the old, the ailing, and the fragile. Many of my client-patients visit me at home, morose because of their situation but after seeing me cheerful despite my overwhelming disability, they start counting their own blessings. You should see how upbeat and confident they are when they go back to their homes after spending some time with me. Today, I have the satisfaction of giving so many people a source of livelihood, too.

What has stood me in good stead always has been my positive attitude towards life. I have always been a social person who loves to interact with people, even strangers. In bus journeys and at airports, while working at my previous job, I would always strike up conversation with people and many of those chance meetings have become long-standing friendships. Today, those very contacts and connections have helped me set up this new venture and I am in a blessed position where I can call up people of influence in my home city if I ever need something resolved or some positive change implemented. Those very contacts have also, sometimes, become my clients. Who does not have an invalid or an ageing relative who requires care?

Looking back, it is my positivity that kept me alive and fighting in the decade after the accident. When the accident happened, the doctors had all pronounced that I would not survive past 72 hours. I told myself that I would prove them wrong and today, here I am, alive and living a fulfilled life, nearly twenty years later.

I never imagined that a single act of reposing faith in myself would lead to something so big and joyful. People tell me I am a source of inspiration to others and often I find myself delivering lectures at schools and colleges where I tell the audience that the only way to live a fulfilled life is to make peace with our realities and find a way to work through them, in order to move on. That is the only way to live. When the Rotary Club of Baroda Cosmopolitan (RCBC) gave me the 'Service Above Self Award' in 2010, it was a reiteration of my belief that we can always find a way forward in life, if we apply our mind to living a life of positivity.

I have never let my disability slow me down in any way. Every once in a while I plan a trip with my family to go see the country. I have travelled in Gujarat, Rajasthan, and other parts of the country. After my daughters got married and had children, I travelled with their families to Shirdi, in Maharashtra, to offer prayers there.

The two decades confined to my wheelchair have resulted in 100 percent calcification of my bones but I have not let even that limit my life. I know I can never walk again or move my body but today, my prayer is that God lets me live this way with no more breakages and surgeries. I am happy in the condition that I am in today.

I have more dreams to give shape to. Having come up close with the plight of the old and the invalid in our country, I dream of setting up an old age home which will give them a welcoming place to live during the waning years of their life. It is a challenging task which requires lot of investment but with a little support, I know I can set up an establishment where those without any support can come and live a happy life. It will be a place where everyone helps and supports each other, and shares their joys and sorrows. Each person who stays there will volunteer in the running of the establishment to the best of their ability because I realize that being a contributing member of society gives a sense of achievement to each of us. Who knows, even this dream of mine might be reality one day....

Suresh Advani

The art uses just three signifiers (a ramp, a staircase, and sun rays) and yet, their inherent symbolic significance and associations between each other open up many possible interpretations.

The focus is on the ramp which could mean that Dr Advani wheeled up on the ramp (quite literally) to the glory of becoming a Padmashri. The ramp also stands for the issue of accessibility and as a turnaround beyond the conventional path, represented by the staircase in the backdrop. Staircase can be seen as difficulties and obstructions posed by mainstream systems and the mindset.

And finally, the rays of sun could be the rays of glory, rays of hope that the Doctor offers to his patients and a beacon of inspiration. Therefore, the sun is left empty and its rays are the ones which are bevelled out.

I am waiting in the 10th floor lobby of Mumbai's Hinduja Hospital, which is where the oncology department is located. Rows upon rows of steel chairs are crammed full of patients and their loved ones and the air is thick with a thousand unsaid feelings—anxiety, fear, frustration, pain, and hope. The silence that hangs in the air is almost unbearable. It is hard not to stare when a young woman comes in, possibly in her mid-20s and what strikes me instantly is not her youthful beauty but the bald pate (obviously from chemotherapy sessions) that she is trying to cover with her saree. Even more difficult to miss is the young man who is with her, shoulders slumped, desperately trying to contain the pain in his eyes.

I sit at the far end of the room, in a row of chairs opposite the lifts that spew an endless stream of patients who head straight for the chairs, unwilling to make eye contact with others who are already there, waiting for their doctors.

When the lift door opens for the nth time, I look up. It is a man who has this brilliant smile on his face that almost contagiously spreads across the room as he swiftly walks past, waving and acknowledging his patients before entering a consultation room. It is only after he has gone that two things strike me. One, the man who just passed by, spreading sunshine, is the famed Dr S.H. Advani, the father of bone marrow transplant in the country and two, that the doctor is wheelchair-bound but no one, including me, seemed to have noticed it.

It is even harder to notice his impairment when I enter the consultation room where he sits behind a table set against the splendid backdrop of the Arabian Sea dancing and sparkling in the background. He is courteous and welcoming but also firm that I have limited time for this conversation because he has to attend to the scores of patients awaiting this attention. And even if it is 5.30 pm, his day is nowhere near ending. He has one more hospital consultancy to attend to before he calls it a day at midnight.

My earliest memories are of growing up with my siblings—3 sisters and a brother—in our modest home in the Mumbai suburb of Ghatkopar. It was a small ground floor apartment, identical to the ninety-nine other ground floor houses that formed a gated community in that town. Like every other Sindhi family of that time, my father went to work and my mother looked after the family. Life was simple and happy—I was good with my academics and spent the rest of my time hanging around in the residential complex, playing with my large group of friends. Everybody knew everybody else in that community and there was never a moment when anyone was lonely.

When I was 8 years old, I came down with a fever that refused to go away. My parents took me to the hospital but by then, it was too late. I had contracted polio and lost the use of my legs. Looking back, I think it must have been a difficult period for my parents because I remember spending 3–4 months at the B.J. Wadia Hospital for Children, which was the only good children's hospital in Mumbai in those days. I don't remember my parents showing me their anxiety or frustration even once in the time I spent at the hospital. What I do remember of my hospital stay was the stream of doctors and nurses who arrived at my bedside at all hours to make sure I was not in pain and discomfort. With my parents beside me and the doctors and nurses who seemed to love me, the hospital stay was far from uncomfortable for me. By the time I was ready to go home, there was a thought in my mind that I wanted to be a doctor too, like the affectionate ones who were looking after all the children in the hospital. The spirit of service, I think, entered my mind when I lay on that hospital bed and continues to drive me to this day.

Back home from the hospital, it was a question of recovering only to some extent; there was no question of regaining full use of my legs ever again but thankfully for me, that never became a problem in my life. I don't know why it happens to some people but I never felt my disability, never felt different from the boy I used to be before my illness. Life went on as before and I continued to go out with my friends who treated me like I was the same boy who hung around with them before. I was able to go to school and study like my siblings did and it made me happy that I scored well in all my exams even if I could not attend school with the same regularity. I was lucky I had teachers who came home for my tuition and friends who also helped me with my lessons, with an extra dose of honesty and affection. When the results of the Secondary School Certificate (SSC) exams were announced, nobody was surprised that I had I stood first in our batch. That was how normal I was perceived to be!

The only difference in my life after I contracted polio was that while I used to run around a lot earlier, I was now moving around on a wheelchair, but I never let that put the brakes on my speed or on my life.

When I finished my 12th grade exams with great scores and the time came for me to make up my mind about my future, medicine was the only thing that I wanted to do. The memory of my hospital stay all those years ago was still fresh in my mind and I kept thinking of the doctors who had treated me with such care and love that I decided I, too, would study to be a doctor and be of service to people.

I encountered the first stumbling block of my disability when I was refused admission to the MBBS course at Grant Medical College even though my marks were high and I was the 6th highest scorer in the first ten shortlisted candidates. Unlike today, when there are centralized exams, in those days, we had to apply for admission in the Mumbai circle.

I went for the admission interview but to my disappointment, I was rejected despite my high scores and performance. I remember being hurt but decided to study Mathematics instead. I continued to be restless about the fact that I could not study medicine so, one day, I sat down and shot off letters to the Prime Minister, the President of India, and the state minister of health, telling them about my plight and bringing the unfairness of it to their notice.

Simultaneously, I was also talking to the deans in medical colleges in Mumbai. I remember approaching the then dean of the college, Dr D V Virkar, and expressing my disappointment to him about the way my candidature was rejected. His response made me more dejected because he said that while he himself was happy to give me admission for MBBS, a panel of other doctors who were on the interview thought I could not do justice to the course. When faced with a joint decision of the panel, Dr Virkar had no choice but to reject my candidature.

Thankfully for me, someone else was looking out for me.

One day Dr Virkar got a call from the office of the state minister of health, instructing him to admit me into the MBBS course (at my own risk!) and he called me in turn, saying that I was welcome to join the course.

I was already one month into my Mathematics course but only too glad to give that up to follow my dream. It was 1965 and I was 18 years old. I think that is where I first started believing in the power of pursuing a dream till it turns into reality.

Over the years, I have often been asked how a teenage boy like me got the courage to write to the Prime Minister of the country and my answer has always been that I was struck by the unfairness of it. I had the marks and deserved to be in that course and even though they had their reasons for rejecting me, I thought it was in my power to do the best that I could to plead my own case.

My years in medical college were a very happy time for me. I went to college and lived a life that was exactly like the rest of my classmates, except that my father provided me an attendant who helped me get around the college in my wheelchair. I went everywhere my classmates went and did all of the things that studying medicine entails– dissections, operations, everything. At the end of the day, I would take a cab back to Ghatkopar and the next morning, I would do it all over again, never tiring or wanting to give up. I think my determination to never be pulled down just came along; I never cultivated it.

In the final year of my MBBS course, I ran into another roadblock when the medical college authorities refused to give me a 'house job' (supervised clinical training sessions that every final year MBBS student has to undergo—a sort of initiation by fire). Not one of the six departments in the college wanted a handicapped person working with them. They neither believed I could cope with the rigorous work on hand nor did they want to take on what they possibly thought would be extra work to manage a person with disability. Once more, a superior force stepped in to protect me in the form of the Professor of medicine, Dr R D Lele, who readily gave me a house job and under the supervision of this kind man and his equally kind assistant, Dr V R Joshi, I went on to do my doctor of medicine (MD) in general medicine. Both of these gentlemen had seen me work hard and grasped my commitment, something the other departmental heads had obviously not noticed. There was a point when my colleagues were advising me to take up pathology, since that would not be too strenuous for me, given my disability. But my mind resisted the thought that I would have to spend my days sitting in a laboratory, looking into a microscope, cut off from the world. I did not want to be in isolation and so it was great then, to get a chance to pursue general medicine.

It was during my MD course that I developed an interest in haematology and oncology, and soon after I completed the course, I started working in the oncology department at the Tata Memorial Hospital in Mumbai. Oncology was not considered a good stream for doctors at that point in time because there was a great gap between what was happening in that field in the West and what was available in India for doctors and patients alike.

But my appetite for knowledge in this space had been whetted and I was hungry for more exposure in developments that were happening in the space in other parts of the world. I started applying for fellowships which was the only way doctors or students could really afford to go abroad and study in those days. I struck gold in 1976, when the Royal Marsden Hospital in London offered me a stint to train with them.

It was a huge step for me professionally and also a milestone, personally. I had never travelled abroad and to be able to spend six months in a foreign country, and having to fend for myself was an intriguing possibility. What also struck me was the fact that when I finally landed there, not a single person remarked on the fact that I was in a wheelchair! It was a soul-fulfilling six months for me because I was hungry for the experience and wanted to lap up everything. Here, I was more of an equal than I had ever been in India and I was expected to participate in everything just as the rest of the team did. It was the first time I had ever been alone but that did not scare me either. There was a lot to learn and that is something that was and continues to be easy for me.

That stay abroad changed me completely. Suddenly, the knowledge that I could travel anywhere in the world, unhindered, opened up a world of possibilities for me. My appetite to travel continues to this day.

Back in India at the Tata Memorial Hospital, I started applying the knowledge that I had gathered at the Royal Marsden. Work was challenging and exciting and I did not know that my personal life was to soon become exciting, too. One day, while doing my rounds at the hospital I came into contact with a lovely young woman who worked there as a nurse. I was a young man at the beginning of my career and spent a lot of time in the wards and therefore, we ran into each other very often. Rosamma (she changed her name to Geeta after we were married) and I soon began spending a lot of our free time together and one day, we decided that we wanted to be together forever. We got married in 1980 and almost immediately, I got my next big break—the opportunity to train and do research at the prestigious Fred Hutchinson Cancer Research Centre in Seattle, in the United States. It was a dream come true for me. It was an eight-month posting for which my wife and I arrived in Seattle, where I discovered that I was one of the fortunate doctors who would get to work with the father of bone-marrow transplant, Dr E Donnall Thomas. He was an icon who was eventually bestowed with the Nobel Prize in medicine in 1990. The centre was a beehive of activity and soon, I was in the thick of bone marrow transplant projects. A group of us discussed cases and observed Dr Thomas at work every day and I was impressed with the team spirit that prevailed there. Everybody from the top to the junior-most member of the team worked together and they were appreciative about the fact that I was able to do all that they were doing, right from the first day.

I maximized my time at the centre, soaking up everything I could about this fascinating new stream that had the potential to save so many lives back in my country. That stay in the US continues to be one of the most memorable phases of my life.

Even when I was getting more and more involved in oncology, there were lots of well-wishers who told me that area had no potential in India. But I already knew that there was a lacuna in treatment available in this field and that there was a latent demand from patients. The stay at Seattle was a transformative phase. The exposure was very good, where I felt I had much more knowledge than I had when I was in India. Bone marrow transplantation was an unheard-of concept in India in 1980. There were a lot of new things that were happening in oncology during those days, which I had now learnt. So I came back and re-joined the Tata Memorial Hospital because, more than anything else, I was attracted by the idea that there was a need for that stream in India and I could do something new in that space. I wanted to be in demand and that appealed to me.

Barely a few months after I arrived back at the Tata hospital, I got the opportunity to practice what I had learnt, when a retired army man from a very modest background approached me for help with his 8-year-old daughter. She had acute myeloid leukaemia and a very slight chance of survival. I wanted to give her a second chance at life and asked her father if he was willing to participate in a first-ever experiment with bone marrow transplantation. I thought he would say no, when he heard this had never been done before in India but his eyes lit up when I told him there was a chance his daughter would survive the disease. His hope fuelled me into action with my team and I quickly getting things organized for the big day. The bone marrow for the transplant was coming from the girl's brother but even so, it was an expensive procedure and since the family was of very modest means, we got to work, begging and borrowing so we could conduct the procedure at the earliest. The team agreed to do the entire process free of charge for her.

At the age of 30, I was on the verge of trying out something path-breaking in cancer treatment. It could have been scary but in my mind I was calm and confident. I had learnt everything I could at Seattle and all I wanted to do was to give life to the precious little girl. For the family, it was like a miracle when we came out of the operation theatre and said we had done the bone marrow transplant successfully. All we had to do now was to wait for three months to make sure it was accepted by the donee. The girl's family had given up hope but three months after the surgery, they realized the set of young doctors had pulled off a miracle and given life new life to their little girl.

That case opened the gates for bone marrow transplants in India. Once we had proved our success with this bold new treatment, lots of other doctors came forward to learn it. Today, bone marrow transplant is practiced successfully all over India and it gives me great satisfaction that I was able to pave the way for that.

For me, the take-away from that first transplant was seeing the entire family come back to life. The grateful father kept in touch with me, visiting me occasionally to keep me updated about his family till he passed away a few years ago. The little girl grew up, studied to be a nurse, and I continue to be in touch with her.

It has been decades since I started my fledgling career and it is remarkable how much progress there has been in medical oncology. When I see that so many types of incurable cancer have now become curable, I am glad I took up this stream of medicine. When I see that some 75 percent of children afflicted with cancer can now survive the disease and go on to lead full lives, it makes me feel blessed that I am among the few people in the country who could help in that process.

People sometimes ask me if I am viewed differently or treated differently by the society because I am disabled. I don't think I am. My experience has been that most people don't even have the time to notice anything about anyone. All these roadblocks and perceptions are the creations of our own mind.

Patients come to me many times feeling bad that they have lost their hair during chemotherapy and I tell them nobody really notices and even if they do, so what? As soon as I say this to them, they go back home, convinced and happy.

When a new patient comes to consult with me, it does not make any difference to him that I am in a wheelchair. Sometimes a patient comes in and when he is on his way out after consultation he says, 'Oh, you are in a wheelchair? I did not even notice!'

We all live in this world so briefly and I want to tell people that it is best to look at things differently, focus on our strengths rather than our weaknesses. Do what you can in the best possible manner instead of moping over what you can't achieve. I am aware that I am in a wheelchair so there is no point aspiring to climb the Himalayas.

Everybody can't do everything. Once you have made peace with that fact, life gets easier for you and everybody around you. Just stick to the things that you are doing well and don't be disappointed or envious that someone else is doing something that you are not able to do. I tell all my patients that a positive mental attitude will always make you see the brighter side of a grim situation. It is all in the mind. Once you have conquered the mind, everything else will seem easy.

My own life is run by one passion: work. To be able to save a life, heal a family, and to do it with complete commitment, is really important for me. Which is why my day starts at 6 am and by the time I call it a day, it is midnight and I have attended to some eighty patients who have waited patiently for my attention in three clinics across different locations in Mumbai. I am fortunate to have a team who assists me in doing this.

From the very beginning, it has been my nature to seek out people and interact with them. I love being with people, love listening to my patients, and sharing their lives. Till a few years ago, I used to travel to other cities, including Delhi, Kolkata, and Jaipur, to consult in hospitals in those cities and I had loved the experience of meeting people from there, too. It gave me enthusiasm and excitement.

They say you learn your best lessons from the experiences that you go through in your own life. My own life changed first time when I lay in that hospital bed at the age of 8, fighting polio.

Three years ago, when I thought I was at the top of everything, my life changed all over again when my 23-year-old daughter died in an accident. She was young, she had just completed her MBBS degree, and had wanted to follow in my footsteps to study medical oncology. I was her hero.

Her death made me introspect. I wished I had been home more often and enjoyed her company instead of following a crazy work schedule. I had never realized that my practice had gotten so busy that I hardly ever spent any time at home. Geeta almost entirely raised our children and looked after the home so that I could further my career goals, never making a fuss about it. My daughter's death changed me in many ways. I have learnt today that we should not take too many things for granted and that we should devote more time to faith in

God. That is what gives you the strength to go on, continue on your chosen path even though it is so difficult to put the past behind you. It was hard for me to forget the dreams of my young child but I had to carry on despite our loss, and it has made me believe in God even more than before. Today, I don't travel to other cities on work but prefer to spend any free time that I have with my wife and son. While my son has chosen his own independent career, Geeta founded Helping Hands, an NGO that helps women detect cancer early and is engaged with cancer patients and their rehabilitation.

I have always believed in God; the existence of someone or something who helps you through your difficulties. My daughter's death made that faith even stronger. I never worry about which God I pray to. It is not important if I pray in a temple, a gurudwara, or a church. It is just important to keep your faith alive.

My life's philosophy is that of service. Give of yourself in the best manner you can and it will always be appreciated. When my patients come back to thank me for having cured them, I am very happy. Sometime they come back after twenty-five years with a loved one who is ailing and when say they trust me to look after that person, it gives me peace.

At airports in unfamiliar cities, someone will come up to me and say hello and say, 'Do you remember me?', and when I don't, they will say, 'Doctor, you treated me so many years ago and I am fine now.' That gives me peace because I know I made a difference in someone's life and that of their family's, too.

Because my work is my all-consuming passion, the thought of retirement never enters my mind. I'll retire in the sense that

I might stop working in clinics, but my knowledge will always be in demand and I plan to put it to good use by setting up a medical institute or a multi-speciality hospital that can be of help to society. That dream is already taking shape in the form of a 250-bed multi-speciality hospital being built in a village in Kerala where my wife grew up. It is still early but I am hoping that the hospital will become the region's first modern hospital. We are dreaming of also setting up an old-age home in the vicinity—the idea is to do something that will alleviate the suffering of human beings. Only then can the knowledge that you have amassed be used in the best possible manner and go on forever.

Acknowledgements

Writing a book is never an effort in isolation. The process of writing is immensely intense and can sometimes be a very lonely process. However, having two authors always helps, in that, there is a give and take of encouragement when the going gets tough and we are each other's watchdogs when there is the temptation to take it easy.

There are countless people—friends, acquaintances, and even complete strangers—who helped us in their own ways to take this book to its logical conclusion and we thank them from their kindness. This book is as much the result of that help as our own efforts.

Archana GS was instrumental in co-ordinating with all the fifteen special people covered in the book. From setting up the interviews to following up on specific asks, her attention to detail helped us focus on the real task of penning the stories.

Nachiket impressed me the first time I saw him making the caricatures for the IIS 2013. When the publisher asked us for sketches for every chapter, I reached out to him and he jumped into the project, coming up with the beautiful impressions that are an integral part of every chapter in this book.

Acknowledgements

Sunil P's research helped *Gifted* in many ways, as did the ideas and connections that he gave us.

Shikha Anand held fort and briefed me on important topics so that I could juggle my multiple hats and still focus on this book.

Arun Sreekumar, Jaideep Rao, Neelanjan Dasgupta and Saurabh Diwan helped us market *Gifted*, an important task because proceeds of this book go to Enable India. Sridhar Sundaram has been my shadow, and alter ego, someone who I turned to for advice, someone whose criticism I worked on and positive feedback I immensely valued.

V. R. Ferose

Sometimes, people meet for a reason. I think I met Ferose because this book was meant to be written. I met him first during the launch events of my debut book, *Leading Ladies*, and later, for the launch of *Legacy* and soon discovered that we shared a lot of common interests. We wrote *Gifted* together because both of us felt strongly that we needed to share the inspirational stories of a section of our population we very often forget to celebrate. Thank you, Ferose, for the shared journey. I learnt a lot from you and from the men and women whose stories we wrote.

Special thanks to my friends, Geeta Kothari and Asha Agarwal, for their priceless contribution to the completion of this book. Geeta gave me unlimited access to her home where I wrote unhindered, plied with great amounts of tea and goodies. Asha Agarwal transcribed my recordings with such speed and dedication that there was no way I could slack off. The book got written on time because the transcriptions landed on my table so fast and furious that I just had to get to work! My best friend and significant other, Prashant, for overlooking the fact that I have largely been missing from our home for the better part of the last year and a half, while I travelled for this book.

My friend Indira Broker kept up her steady encouragement, connected me with her niece, Shilpa Zaveri, who then connected me with a few of her connections who have featured in this book. Alka Kshirsagar refused to let me give up when I was exhausted and talked about giving up my writing bug. 'This is who you are and you owe it to yourself to write,' she told me. I am grateful to all of them for their generosity and for their faith in me.

We interviewed a lot of sterling men and women whose stories do not appear in this book. Nupur Jain, Kartik Varun Chadha, Shobha, Major D P Singh, Orko Roy, Arzan Patel, Vinod Rawat, Ruchir Falodia—your stories inspired us and gave us a fresh new perspective about living life with a disability. Your stories are not in this book but you have left your indelible mark on its soul.

Thanks to Milee Ashwarya for believing in this book and adopting it as her very own, Gurveen Chadha for editing it with love and care, and to Caroline Newbury and Shruti Katoch for promoting this very special book in a very special way.

Sudha Menon

Acknowledgements

In the end, we are grateful for the love, the unconditional support, and the patience of our families for forgiving us for the no-shows at special family occasions. They understood this was a precious project about precious people whose stories needed to be told. And when it was complete, they were to first to read it and applaud. We owe you all big time.

A Note on the Authors

Sudha Menon is the author of two bestselling non-fiction books, *Leading Ladies: Women Who Inspire India*, and *Legacy*, a compilation of letters from inspirational Indian men and women to their daughters. She is a former newspaper journalist and is currently a columnist.

Sudha is the founder of Get Writing!, a writing workshop that she set up to help people kick start their writing journey and is founder of Writing In the Park, an initiative to get people to explore their creativity while writing in public parks and gardens.

Sudha is a TEDx speaker and often speaks at educational institutions and corporate campuses about women's leadership and diversity issues.

Meeting the people she interviewed and wrote about in *Gifted* made her realize the immense potential and promise that each of us carry within us. Some of us manage to tap that well deep within us to bring out our best while some go through life without the faintest idea of who we can really be. Having met the people in *Gifted*, she is determined to live her life to the fullest, just as they do.

V.R. Ferose is Senior Vice President and Head of Globalization Service for SAP AG and former Managing Director of SAP Labs India.

Deeply sensitive to the unequal world in which we live, Ferose founded the 'India Inclusion Summit', a unique platform that focuses on the need for inclusion in our lives. He is a Director on the Board of Specialist People Foundation, a not-for-profit foundation with the goal to create one million jobs globally for people with autism and is on the panel of 'The Vision Group on Information Technology', Government of Karnataka. He is also co-founder of the Karnataka chapter of Global Shapers, which works to create leadership among the youth.

For his professional accomplishments, commitment to society, and potential to contribute to shaping the future of the world, Ferose was honored as a 'Young Global Leader' in March 2012 by the World Economic Forum. In a study published by the *Economic Times* and Spencer Stuart, Ferose was selected as one of the leaders in 'Indian's Top 40 under 40', 2014. This study is considered to be India's most authentic leadership study and it lists 40 extraordinary business leaders under the age of 40.

For more information on the book, please visit the website: http://www.giftedthebook.com/